Transformed by Love

Dedicated
with love and gratitude
to
three fathers in God

the late Reverend Donovan Victor Evening
(who was also my natural father)

the Right Reverend Cuthbert Bardsley
(former Bishop of Coventry)

the Most Reverend Doctor Khotso Walter Paul Makhulu
(Archbishop of Central Africa)

Transformed by Love

The Way of Mary Magdalen

MARGARET MAGDALEN CSMV

Foreword by Jean Vanier

Darton, Longman and Todd
London

First published in 1989 by
Darton, Longman and Todd Ltd
89 Lillie Road, London SW6 1UD

© 1989 Sister Margaret Magdalen CSMV

British Library Cataloguing in Publication Data

Margaret Magdalen *Sister*, CSMV
  Transformed by love
  1. Bible. N.T. Mary, Magdalen, Saint
  I. Title
  225.9′24

  ISBN 0–232–51816–5

Phototypeset by Input Typesetting Ltd, London
Printed and bound in Great Britain by
Anchor Press Ltd, Tiptree, Essex

Contents

Jesus receive my heart, and bring me to Thy love:
all my desire Thou art, and Thy coming I covet . . .

Thou art He whom I have sought, when shall I see Thy
Face?

Richard Rolle

Foreword

This book has touched me deeply. Sister Margaret Magdalen gave the manuscript to me at a time when Mary of Bethany – Mary Magdalen – was becoming very important to me in my life. I was beginning to realise that in some way she was the key to a mystery of love. Her radical poverty, her immense passion and love, her audacity in her love, were a gift *from* Jesus and also a consolation for his heart. When the apostles were quibbling amongst themselves (as men often do) when fear, disillusion or despair had taken hold of them, Mary was firmly, decidedly, unshakenly, passionately in love with Jesus, glued to him. And her love, her immense love, consoled his wounded heart.

In our world today, where there is so much quibbling amongst Christians, Mary Magdalen has something to teach us: 'Be in love with Jesus. Be attached to him and to his Word firmly, decidedly, unshakenably, passionately. Don't get caught up in the despair of our world. Trust and give all!' And, of course, she could only love as she loved because she knew that she herself was loved by Jesus firmly, infinitely, tenderly and mercifully.

This Mary is a hidden figure. When Matthew and Mark speak of her breaking the flask of precious ointment and pouring it on the head of Jesus just before his death, they say that Jesus spoke solemnly about this 'beautiful' act: 'Wherever the gospel is preached in the whole world, what she has done will be told in memory of her' (Matthew 26:13). But strangely enough they do not mention her

name. However, the evangelist John, writing possibly
twenty years after the others, breaks the silence. He tells
us clearly who the woman is and the part she plays in the
tragic and beautiful story of the passion of Christ. Jesus
performed the miracle of the resurrection of Lazarus in
answer to the pain and tears of Mary (John 11:33–6). As
Mary wept, Jesus also wept. He loved her so deeply. His
heart responded to her cry. He had said 'Ask and you shall
receive' (Luke 11:9). She asked through tears. He answered
through tears. And the resurrection of Lazarus was the
determining factor in the decision of the High Priest and
Elders to do away with Jesus (John 11:53). The gospel of
John is eminently clear about this. In this light, we can
understand the great passion and love of Mary for Jesus
and why she poured the very costly ointment over his head
and feet 'wasting so much money'.

This ardent, loving woman – who did not care what
people said about her – was certainly at the Cross,
continuing to love him. She is surely that same ardent
woman who, early on the morning of the third day, went to
the tomb. The same woman to whom Jesus first appeared,
sending her to tell the apostles that he was alive.

Sister Margaret Magdalen follows her heart and her
deep intuition. Despite reputed biblical scholars who see
Mary of Magdala, Mary of Bethany and the sinful woman
of Luke 10 as three different people, Sister Margaret
Magdalen suggests that they may have been one and the
same woman. A woman in love with Jesus. A woman who
had touched the depths of abjection, despair and distress.
A woman whose body had been soiled through prostitution.
A woman excluded and excommunicated from the Jewish
communion. A woman who thus, in despair, had become
possessed by seven devils. But a woman who had been
loved and transformed by Jesus. He had looked at her and
loved her. His piercing, loving eyes had seen through the
crust of her despair and awoken the little light burning in
the depths of her being. No wonder she loved with passion.

And it is this broken and healed woman who anoints the feet of Jesus in Bethany and is the first to meet the risen Christ and become the apostle of apostles.

When I read Sister Margaret Magdalen's manuscript, my heart was touched, because my intuition was the same as hers. Mary Magdalen, has something very important to say about love to the Church and to our world today. So when I was asked to write the Foreword to Sister Margaret Magdalen's book, I could not say no. I felt so much in communion with her, not just with her thought, but with her spirituality and her heart. I felt one with her in her love for Mary.

Since reading this manuscript, some writings by the French Dominican Father Philippe Devoucoux du Buysson have been given to me. Father Devoucoux du Buysson is at present the Father Guardian of the Grotto of the Saint Baume in southern France. Tradition has it that Mary spent the last years of her life in the Grotto which has been a place of pilgrimage for many years. Father Devoucoux du Buysson has meditated on Mary during the past few years and has lived spiritually alongside her. In a series of booklets he presents an extremely rich teaching on Mary, drawing on biblical sources – especially the Greek texts – on sound theology and astute psychological insights. He comes to the same conclusion.

> At the end of this study, I have come to a deep conviction that Mary Magdalen, the sister of Martha and Lazarus, and the woman having seven devils [St Luke] are one and the same person. I know, however, that the debate around this question is not closed. I would call my convictions very highly probable.*

I was strengthened and consoled by these manuscripts. They confirmed that Sister Margaret Magdalen's intuitions

---

* *Les Cahiers de la Sainte Baume*, no. 1, 1988, Association Dominicana, 9 Rue St François de Paule, 06000, Nice.

and my own were not just on the spiritual level. They were not only rooted in the liturgy and long-standing devotion throughout the ages, but in sound theological and biblical studies.

This book is not a biblical or theological reflection; it is a book of spirituality, which calls us to love more passionately, to cry out our sorrow more acutely, and to integrate our brokenness more fully. It calls us to grow through love and to celebrate relationships, especially our relationship with the risen Jesus. Sister Margaret Magdalen shows us the road Mary Magdalen took. Mary is a wonderful model who can teach us to walk more surely on the road of Jesus. Although she is a biblical scholar, Sister Margaret Magdalen has not learned all this from written sources. It is obvious that she has also been formed and led by Jesus and by his Holy Spirit. And I believe that she has learned a great deal from the poor, the weak and the fragile, for she has spent a number of years in Africa, close to people in poverty, and lived for a while with people who are handicapped. This book will nourish our hearts, our minds and our love, and if we read it slowly, prayerfully, meditatively, it will help us to become better followers of Jesus.

l'Arche   Jean Vanier
Trosly-Breuil
France

Acknowledgements

It is never possible, in a list of acknowledgements, to give due credit to each person who has contributed in some way to the production of a book, and whose influence and help are reflected in its pages. Always, of course, there are many hidden influences of which even the author is not fully aware – through reading, through encounters, through conversations, through teaching and discussion down through the years.

Nevertheless, I must attempt to make some specific, even if inadequate, acknowledgements and, in doing so, to express my thanks publicly to those who have given particular help in this venture.

Although he would possibly have found it surprising, such was his humility, I should like to record my deep gratitude and life-long debt to the late Charles Jupe, former English Master of Purbrook Park Grammar School, Hants for thirty-two years. A brilliantly gifted teacher, his intellectual honesty and discipline were unforgettable, and his influence on all his pupils profound. Out of the many and grateful memories I have of him, the most enduring is that of the man himself, his warmth and kindness. Some words of encouragement and praise from him (never given lightly or insincerely) first set me on the path of writing, and I hereby gladly record my indebtedness to him, over forty years later.

The initial inspiration for this book came from Teresa de Bertodano, of Darton, Longman and Todd, who drew out most of the ideas in conversation and then waited patiently, for over two years, till I was free to put them on paper. I am grateful to her for prompting me to write in the first place, and her subsequent encouragement.

Sincere thanks also go to Kerry and Tony Schüssel who gave me very gracious hospitality in their home here in Gaborone, and the much needed space and quiet in which to write; to Joyce Knightley, Oblate of the Community of St Mary the Virgin, who lives and works with the Sisters of our Provincial Mother House in Irene, South Africa, for her generous offer to type the manuscript (which includes deciphering my handwriting) and for the speed and professionalism with which she did it, and to Kerry Schüssel, who assisted with the typing of one chapter; to my Community, particularly Sister Gillian Ruth and the late Sister Irene Benedict for checking references, to Sister Elizabeth Mary for help in the final stages and to the Sisters here in Botswana for giving me freedom to write and supporting me in the process. I am also extremely grateful to Sister Bridget Mary CSMV who introduced me to Katharine Watson's poem.

I acknowledge the particular help of Matthew Fox SJ in his book *Original Blessing*, and for the confidence it gave me to pursue certain lines of thought in mine. I found much of what he wrote resonating with my own less well articulated thinking, and challenging me to clarify it. I am grateful, too, for much that was new and enriching and for permission from Bear & Co., P.O. Drawer 2860 Santa Fé, New Mexico, to quote from the book.

Almost all the Scripture quotations are from the Revised Standard Version of the Bible, copyrighted 1971 and 1952 by the Division of Christian Education of the National Council of the Churches of Christ in the USA. For permission to quote Katherine Watson's 'Easter Hymn – to St Mary Magdalen' from *The Source and Other Poems* I am grateful to Oxford University Press. I am also grateful to Faber and Faber Ltd for permission to quote two extracts from *Collected Poems 1909–1962* by T. S. Eliot and to Macmillan Ltd for permission to quote from *Frequencies* by R. S. Thomas.

Lastly, I must add a very special and personal word of gratitude for Mary Magdalen, herself. My devotion to her dates back to a time long before I received the habit of the Community of St Mary the Virgin and took her name. It is her passionate love of the Lord and ardent following of him with which I seek to identify ever more closely as the years pass.

Gaborone   Sister Margaret Magdalen CSMV
Botswana

Easter Hymn – to St Mary Magdalen

She, Mary, who extravagantly broke
Her costly treasure, alabaster box,
She, Magdalen,
In desolation in that early dawn
Seeking in secret, seeking out the tomb,
Somehow, someway, her sorrow to assuage,
She, Magdalen, she in the garden saw,
She first, she – ah! – the Resurrection saw.
And spoke, she first of all,
Rabboni, Lord, her heartbreak and her love.
                                    And then –
The April rain, the morning sun, and joy
And joy and joy and overmastering joy
Of love accepted, love returned to earth
In lilies no more Lenten, birds
All Glory, Glory, Glory calling, she
Alone quite speechless for her pain,
Her not to be appeasèd pain, of love,
The everlasting Easter of the heart.

Katherine Watson

Introduction

It will be obvious, from the name in Religion given to me when I received the habit of our Community, why I was drawn to the subject of 'Mary Magdalen'. Yet, it was not purely, or chiefly, out of personal devotion to her that this book was written.

Hers was a life which encompassed so many of the crises and growth points that we all meet in our journey to God, that reflection upon it must surely yield a rich harvest of inspiration. Here then, like a lens focusing light, I pray she will reveal to us something of the amazing grace in a relationship with Jesus, and the sheer power of passion, penitence, fervour, faith and freedom, which we, too, can discover if we are prepared for her kind of ardent commitment.

What information do we actually have about this woman who makes such a strong impact in the Gospels? It is surprisingly little, and yet, that little is enough to create a vividly powerful impression.

She had been healed by Jesus of demonic possession (Mark 16:9; Luke 8:2). She was one of the women who followed him from Galilee (Luke 8:2), who stood at the foot of the cross (Luke 23:55; John 19:25), accompanied the body of Jesus to the tomb in Joseph's garden and sat over against it whilst the Roman guard sealed the sepulchre (Matt. 27:61, 66; Mark 15:47; Luke 23:55). She joined the other women (whose names vary in the different accounts) and went to the tomb, carrying spices, early in the morning 'on the first day of the week' (Matt. 28:1; Mark 16:2; Luke

24:10; John 20:1ff) to complete the customary burial rituals.

In Matthew's account, Mary and another Mary meet the risen Lord as they return from the tomb (Matt. 28:1-10). In John's account, however (John 20:1-18), she was at one point *alone* at the tomb, weeping, when Jesus appeared to her in risen form, and commissioned her to break the news of his resurrection to the other disciples – which she did. According to Luke, they would not accept her testimony and dismissed it as an 'idle tale' (Luke 24:11).

Biblically speaking that is where the information ends. Traditionally and liturgically, however, the portrait of Mary Magdalen has been a composite picture of several women.

She is often associated in people's minds with the woman who anointed Jesus with costly perfume in the house of Simon the Pharisee (Matt. 26:6-13; Mark 14:3-9; Luke 7:36-50), thereby showing her gratitude and devotion. This was the woman who is described as a 'sinner' (technical terminology for a prostitute) which has led to the supposition that Mary was a woman with a bad reputation.

It is sometimes suggested that she might have been the unnamed woman caught in the act of adultery who was dragged before Jesus and totally forgiven by him (John 8:3-11).

The reference to Mary of Bethany as the one who 'anointed the Lord with ointment, wiping his feet with her hair' (John 11:3) has caused some to wonder if she is the same woman who entered the Pharisee's house and broke her precious alabaster box of perfume over Jesus – a woman who as we have seen has also been identified by some as Mary Magdalen. That would imply that Mary of Bethany and Mary Magdalen were one and the same person.

Critically speaking that is unlikely and poses many questions, but for the purposes of this book, I have followed the liturgical tradition which draws upon most of the stories to which I have referred. Since this is a book for devotional reflection, it seemed inappropriate to enter into detailed *critical* arguments as to the identities of these several women whose stories run parallel, overlap and sometimes merge. The composite picture of Mary Magdalen provides us with a not inauthentic icon to lead us deeper into the mysteries of God's transfiguring work in human life.

I use the word 'icon' quite deliberately. A religious painting, carving or sculpture, may grant us insights through the fairly subjective perceptions and interpretation of the artist. In iconography, however, there are rules to be observed and a necessary obedience to recognised signs and symbols, complementarity of shape and meaning in colour – all of which give a certain objectivity. The icon is not a holy picture but a window. It is intended to draw the worshipper into a divine mystery, into some particular aspect of the being of God.

It was my intention through the chapters of this book to see how Mary Magdalen could become such a window and, through the particular aperture of her own experience, to lead us out into broader issues of spirituality. She draws us into the mysteries of creation and re-creation, redemption of matter, conversion of life and transfiguration.

Chapter 1, therefore, is an attempt to explore the inter-relatedness of earthiness and holiness, the need to own and rejoice in the gifts of passion, sexuality, being 'earthed' in this world and finding God in all things. Many of us need to be set free in these areas and delivered from bondage to a dualism which still bedevils the Western Church. The very word 'passion' needs to be rescued from its negative connotations, enlarged beyond the particular sense of suffering, and placed in the perspective of celebration. Mary Magdalen points the way to a powerful, earthy yet holy drive, an energy sanctified by love. In Magdalen, we do not find discarnate desires. Earth, body and senses are all potential vehicles of the holy and whole life in which the Spirit of Jesus is incarnated.

Chapter 2 centres on the life-changing power in penitence, the experience of total acceptance within forgiveness and the transfiguration of failure. We may know this very well at head level but it needs a constant reiteration at heart level as we learn to accept our weaknesses, our shadow side, the 'stuff' of which we have been made and the experiences which have formed us. The door of hope does not swing open automatically. It follows upon deep penitence, the tears of which dip us again in God till we are new-created.

Chapter 3 explores the unselfconscious fervour, the all-or-nothingness of the love of the Lord which springs from personal encounter, through a radical experience of forgiveness, and through a reckless devotion that is frequently misunderstood and labelled 'crazy'. This chapter also seeks to enter into Mary Magdalen's feelings *as a woman* – especially where her spontaneity in expressing love was hampered by convention – and what this may still have to say to us today about feminine expressions of piety.

Chapter 4 takes us into an area of spirituality which none of us is able to avoid or escape if we are to mature in the life of prayer. In Mary Magdalen we see our own desperation reflected. The dread of loss, the fear of journeying in the dark, the bewilderment in the seeming absence of the Lord, the unwillingness to venture out on to new frontiers in our relationship with him, were all Magdalen's experience, too. We cling fearfully to all that spells security. Yet, as we dare to let go, indeed embrace the dark, we find the Lord we thought we had lost in new and radical ways.

Chapter 5, therefore, leads on from that fear to discover, with Magdalen, what freedom can be found when we dare to heed the words of Jesus, 'Don't cling'. A clinging in any relationship cramps it, until one or other person feels trapped. When we set each other free and allow one another growing-space, then we learn what it is to 'dance' together evolving new patterns for growth. What Mary Magdalen discovered at the mouth of that cavernous tomb

– which opened on to the abyss of her horror, the grave of her hopes and memories – we all discover as we pursue with fidelity our calling to prayer. The Lord constantly voids our preconceived expectations, surprises us, comes to us from behind (when we are facing in the wrong direction), gently loosens our fear-filled grip on the known and understood, and goes before – ever before – dancing ahead, touching the earth lightly and lovingly and beckoning us to join him. He will not be bound by grave clothes, or anything else other than love. He calls us on to freedom and joy in a passionate, holistic and holy life.

1

Celebration of Earthiness

The power of passion

A saint is not pure spirit. He may not be mistaken for an angel: even death cannot make him one. For holiness belongs primarily to this world. It bears witness that the life we live on earth, a bodily life with all its weakness and pettiness, is yet capable of receiving the rays of supernatural light and of taking on a new and transcendent meaning. This teaches us not merely to endure life, but to desire and even to love it. . . . The saint may mortify his passions, but they remain a condition and even an element of his holiness. For holiness is itself a passion. . . .

(Louis Lavelle)[1]

God, far from being put off by our sensuality, 'is in our sensuality'. We are to treat our sensuality and earthiness kindly and harmoniously, for they are 'founded in nature, in compassion and in grace'.

(Matthew Fox sj)[2]

A woman came in, who had a bad name in the town. . . . She waited behind him at his feet, weeping, and her tears fell on his feet, and she wiped them away with her hair; then she covered his feet with kisses and anointed them with the ointment.

(Luke 7:37–8)

How embarrassing – this unwarranted display of emotion, this uninhibited splurging out of passion, this inappropriate expression of gratitude and affection! Surely there must be a more acceptable, socially recognised and properly ordered means of giving thanks? Less obtrusive, less physical, less hysterical ways of demonstrating love?

So might the men have felt as they watched this woman pouring out her ointment, her tears and her devotion upon the feet of the one who had revolutionised her life.

We know from the Scriptures that they were critical – about the expense of this gesture, the waste of something that could be valued in monetary terms. But underneath their objections – the cerebral, logical arguments – what were they really saying? Was it not something arising from an attitude prevalent then but which has continued into the Christian Church and dogged us down through the ages? Was it not a fear of passion? – or, at least, of passion demonstrated? When passion is expressed in physical gesture, and moreover publicly, then it is simply 'not on'. Not in Christian worship. Those who have allowed their passion greater freedom and expression than was perhaps the norm have often found themselves outcasts. They have shocked and offended their churches, given rise to distaste and disease amongst its leaders and people, and have therefore proved a source of irritation and embarrassment.

In the eighteenth century, the Church of England could not cope with John Wesley's fiery zeal – the outcome of that life-changing experience in Aldersgate Street when his heart became strangely kindled and a fire was lit within him which became a mighty blaze spreading across England.

He is only one of many, as wide-ranging in character and time as Billy Bray and Francis of Assisi, whose passionate response to Jesus could not be contained within the normal structures, who were shocking without intending to be so, and who touched on that very raw nerve of fear – the fear of being unable to handle so powerful a force as passion. Fear warns us, 'It might all get out of control.' Such a fear is the substance of many a nightmare. We are terrified of the 'Pandora's box' of our emotions which, once opened, will spill out in a totally, uncontrollable way. We must certainly never allow this to happen in worship, we tell ourselves. Indeed, all too often, when it comes to worship, we feel the need to keep emotion under wraps. Things must be done decently and in order, with dignity, liturgical rectitude, in accordance with tradition and custom, and above all, with blessed moderation.

So, we have dammed up our tears, stifled our spontaneity and curbed the Charismatics. We have applied reason and even cynicism to the 'unusual' – the miraculous healings, the spontaneous outburst of song, the welling up of the heart and the desire to share the resulting joy. We have applied restraint within ourselves and upon others. We have tried to confine boundless joy and reduce it to manageable proportions. We have, quite simply, quenched the Spirit by allowing ourselves to become prisoners to our own fear.

I am not knocking dignity in worship. There is a right place for order, tidiness and professionalism in worship. Many of us appreciate being able to relax into the smooth-running predictability of a set pattern. It can be beautiful and God-honouring – for God is a God of order and not of confusion. However, dignified worship is not necessarily devoid of passion. Like water, passion can be channelled as much in deep, underground rivers as in spectacular waterfalls.

These days we are able to watch major ceremonial occasions on TV – from royal weddings to papal visits, from midnight masses to the dedication of cathedrals. The rich blend of colour, sound and movement, the impeccable timing, the attention to every detail, the precision of the processions all lead us into deep, if quiet, worship. Ceremonial has always been of the essence of worship and is not a happy bed-fellow of a casual, anything-goes approach.

Perhaps the formal occasion appeals very especially to some but formality and dignity are only partial reflections of the divine image within us. We also share in the creatorship of one who goes in for profusion and sponta-neity. That part of our divinity we tend to neglect or even deny. Somehow we feel ashamed of it and deeply fearful.

Our need to keep a firm hand on the controls dominates.
Yet, as Annie Dillard puts it,

> The extravagant gesture is the very stuff of creation.
> After the one extravagant gesture of creation in the first
> place, the universe has continued to deal exclusively in
> extravagances, flinging intricacies and colossi down
> aeons of emptiness, heaping profusions or profligacies
> with ever fresh vigour. The whole show has been on fire
> from the word go!'[3]

How refreshing, then, is this woman, Mary Magdalen,
who comes with her spontaneous, disorderly gesture of
love, who makes no attempt to trim her action to contemporary norms of behaviour, who is unafraid to touch, or
to use symbols and actions that were certainly open to
misunderstanding and disapproval.

We so often seek to worship God with our hearts, our
souls and our minds and leave the body somewhere out on
the fringe. The Hebrew didn't fall into this dichotomy. He
didn't divide himself into soul and body – he was one.
'Heaven *and earth* are full of your glory' we sing, and with
his holistic approach, the Jew saw no false distinction
between the heavenly and the earthly. His is an attitude
we need to recover – or, maybe, discover for the first time.
For, 'to be holy is not to be heavenly, but to know God in
one's earthiness and in one's flesh'.[4] Or, as Hildegarde of
Bingen puts it: 'Holy persons draw to themselves all that
is earthly. . . .'[5]

Humility derives from the word *humus*, meaning earth,
so Meister Eckhart has pointed out. Part of humility, therefore, is being in touch with the earth, rejoicing in and
befriending our own earthiness, celebrating the blessing
that our earthiness, our sensuality and passions are. 'To
deny our earthiness is to bottle up deep and divine energies
of creativity and imagination.'[6] Consider the loss there has
been to mankind down the ages through such damming
up! Most of us must have found ourselves singing at some

time or other words such as: 'From earthly passions set me free and make me pure within,'[7] and we have understood very well what was implied. We were praying to be freed from the grip of those self-seeking, ego-building, self-gratifying desires that would manipulate others by the misuse of power. We ask to be released from bondage to that which is greedy, grasping and subhuman in our appetites, to be raised to the true dignity of our humanity. But sadly, in shunning the wrongful *use* of passion, we have at times tried to eliminate the passion itself. The Christian life has then been seen as one from which all passion has been squeezed out leaving it like a dried-up lemon. And yet, 'there is in passion a power that holiness needs'.[8] We have a long history of false thinking to overcome. Many of the early Fathers saw the struggle for holiness as a clamp down on our base, earthly passions, a mortification of our senses. Thomas à Kempis, for example, refers fourteen times in the *Imitation of Christ* to the need to fight against passions, get rid of them, be free from them, cease to be weighed down by them or oppressed by the many evil ones which lurk below the surface of our conscious (my words, not his). He speaks of passion being 'unsubdued' and 'ill-regulated'. But he never speaks of it as a God-given gift or blessing.

Within the monastic tradition there has in the past been much teaching on the subduing of desires – at one time even bringing them into subjection by the use of the *flagellus*. For some the vow of celibacy, far from being a freeing thing, almost encouraged a denial of sexuality. Paul himself spoke of bringing his body (with its appetites) into subjection and of gaining mastery over this powerful machine which we all seem to blame for leading us into sin – except Jesus, of course. He didn't denigrate poor Brother Ass. He pointed out that sin began in the mind and in the heart. The body was merely instrumental in executing the sin.

Passion is, of course, rooted in the will but expressed

through the body. But, since converted passion is a form of holiness, then the body itself cannot be antipathetic to holiness. It is *out* of the body, out of the earthiness, out of the senses of the whole man that holiness rises up. 'There is nothing finer than to see the fire which feeds the most base materials produce at its highest point a flame radiating so great a light.'⁹

Meister Eckhart's image is perhaps even more vivid. Instead of trying simply to control and subdue passions as one would an untamed horse, he suggests that we put on them 'the bridle of love'. They still retain, therefore, their original energy and they are not stifled out of existence. Instead, the bridle, steering them, making them work for us as *we* choose, becomes a way of harnessing their energy and potential for positive rather than destructive purposes. It frees them to give birth to ever-deepening compassion and moral outrage, to lead us into areas where we need, but fear, to go. Then indeed they can be cause for celebration. What need is there for shame, for masking or disguising this blessing when it is 'bridled by love'? Yet for many of us, it may be a life-time's work to get rid of the dualism in our thinking, the deeply rooted sense that there is a hostile relationship between our bodies and souls, that animal and spirit are strongly opposed to each other, that to be holy is to deny our sensuality.

One good reason for focusing on Mary Magdalen as an icon penetrating certain spiritual mysteries is that she succeeded where many of us fail. She seems to have reached an inner harmony where passion was converted or 'bridled by love', rather than denied, imprisoned, repressed or beaten out of the body (if that were ever possible!).

She who once used her earthiness in a way that dishonoured her sexuality, destroying true relationship and turning passion into lust, now allowed that same down-to-earthiness to provide a channel for her love. The burning passion she now felt for Jesus *had* to find an outlet of expression, for 'love must be made real in act, as desire unites with desired'.[10]

Here was *pure* passion, fervent desire, expressed in a very overt, bodily contact, but untinged by lust, unspoiled by attention-seeking. For lust is always self-centred, greedy, grasping, out for its own ends, abusive and demeaning – whether it is lust for power, lust for money, sexual lust, lust for possessions or lust for prestige. It is dominated by the 'I want, therefore I must have' attitude, without thought or concern for those who are manipulated by its evil force. Other people become objects, means to the end which is solely self-gratification. There is no humility in lust and therefore no true earthiness, no honouring of the other, no cause for rejoicing, no deepening into compassion. Lust is a cheat, a deceiver, an arid thing. It holds out hollow promises that are nothing but mockery and lead to disillusionment.

Lust has only to do with self and ends in self-destruction whereas passion (by derivation) has to do with an ability to suffer and ends in sacrificial love. All passion leads to a mixture of joy and sorrow. The more passionately we love, the more vulnerable we become. It was the passion of love that led Mary the mother of Jesus and Mary Magdalen to stand at the foot of the Cross, sharing in the passion of *Christ's* love as he gave himself for the world and its redemption.

So then, the energy of passion in Mary which had previously been so foully misused and abused, is now converted. It does not as a result lessen in power. Indeed, like channelling water, the diverting of it towards Jesus increases its power, for the love, which is reciprocated, is both life-giving and energising.

In Christ all our lust can be taken up, converted, re-made and transformed. Hence, Mary was free in herself to touch Jesus, weep over his feet, dry them with her hair, kiss them and anoint them.

Underneath the seemingly reasonable objections given

by the onlookers, were these actions an uncomfortable evoking of memories for some of them? Did they find themselves recalling other occasions when *they* had been on the receiving end of similar treatment but in a very different context? Was it all a bit too near the bone to be able to cope with a replay of such experiences?

Whatever the reasons, they found Mary's behaviour absolutely shocking. What right had she to come barging in – on a male occasion – and force her attention upon Jesus, flagrantly performing an action which could have been, and undoubtedly was, interpreted as being full of sexual overtones.

But Jesus understood – completely. He knew the heart that motivated the action. He saw the purity of converted passion in Mary at that moment – a passion into which she could integrate her sexuality in a wholesome and holy way.

Little did these men realise how soon Jesus himself would be performing a similar action in wiping *their* feet. Little did they dream how near was the time when he would be showing his love in the same demonstrable way and, in a new commandment, urging them to love one another!

There seem to be all too many Christians who are unable to come to terms with, let alone celebrate, their earthiness; they are trapped in a way of thinking that cannot deal with the holiness of sexuality. Many cannot grasp that they block God's transforming power in their lives when they refuse to face up to and integrate this powerful side of their nature. As Peter Dodson says, 'I think I have reached the view that most of the trouble stems from the sad and persistent confusion that exists between sexuality and genitality. It is a confusion which blocks many expressions of loving desire: the language of love, the look of love, the touch of love.'[11]

Sexuality is an essential part of being human and a cause for rejoicing. If we try to ignore or somehow deny it, we distance ourselves from God who is truth. Part of our growth in God is becoming more real, and reality demands

that we face up to what it means to be man or woman –
a sexual being. If we attempt to repress our sexuality by
refusing or fearing to accept it, then it will break out in
various undesirable, ugly ways such as jealousy, moodi-
ness, withdrawal, domination, ruthless oppression, materi-
alism, passive docility, crushes, unhealthy dependence, etc.

All human beings have within them elements of both
sexes, and wholeness implies accepting the opposites within
ourselves – cultivating one's feminity (the Anima) as a
man, and one's masculinity (the Animus) as a woman.[12]
Wholeness also implies accepting that we are incomplete,
that we shall experience the ache of longing for the other
half. By that ache we are reminded that the image of God
is not to be found in man *or* woman but in the two together
– in the complementariness of their relationship. Some
while ago, Gilbert Russell wrote,

> Mankind is made man–woman: the great tree is split at
> the root. God at the instant of creation, divided the race
> in two. 'Male and female created he them.' From this
> great wound the body of man aches and will ache to the
> end. Sex is the standing problem which can never merely
> be 'solved'. It is set in the flesh and blood and the quick
> matter of life and mind, and can only be healed. The
> wound is healed in marriage – in every marriage; but in
> no marriage perfectly, and in some hardly at all.[13]

True as this is, it is not the whole truth. The wound
may be healed partly outside of marriage, in friendships,
in spiritual bonds with people of either sex, and in
community life. Ultimately of course, we find our
completion in God himself.

We have to be real, however, and admit in all honesty
that we have not reached that point yet. We may not be
able to sing with full conviction. 'Thou, O Christ, art all
I want, more than all in Thee I find . . .'[14] This is all right.
It is being real. It is admitting that we are on a journey –
a journey of growth in God and into completeness in God

but we are not 'there' yet. We have not reached *teleios*, which is rather misleadingly translated as 'perfect' in most versions of Matthew's Gospel. However, when we are enjoined to 'be perfect as your Heavenly Father is perfect', it is not in the sense of moral perfection or total lack of imperfection.

We are called to be *teleios* in the sense of being mature, full-grown, adult, complete. It is part of maturity to accept and own that we have quite a way to go towards completeness, that we have to struggle to love purely, that we still experience the searing ache of imperfection.

We should also say in this context that, today in an alarming way, the wound of incompleteness, far from being helped is deepening in many a marriage. For some people marriage brings deep loneliness, an ever-increasing emptiness and a loss of self-worth. To find that you are not the 'other half' as you thought, but the other 'third' or 'quarter' is devastating. To discover that the 'first love' has grown cold or been replaced by another 'love', whether it be a thing, a person, or work, is heart-breaking. The trust that is blown apart by infidelity, the trauma of divorce or separation, the splitting of the family, the sharing of custody of the children, the humiliation of crashing hopes and the pain of breaking hearts, the meaninglessness of sex isolated from its proper context of an ongoing commitment, all leave lasting and terrible wounds. Our society is becoming more and more wounded every day. We are 'sick unto death' in this respect. The attraction to another partner may seem to be sexual, but might it not, at root, stem from a hunger for respect, affirmation or tenderness – perhaps insufficiently expressed in the marriage? We can only begin the way back to healing by recognising the proper needs of our sexuality rather than heeding the demanding voice of sex alone.

The integration of our sexuality implies an acceptance of our place as we see it in the complementariness of the man/woman relationship in society as a whole – which is different from accepting a role imposed *upon* us, as women by men, for example, or vice versa! It is to rejoice in the particular and unique contributions we are able to make as women or as men and to see ourselves as gift.

It implies being at home in our bodies, rejoicing in the marvel that they are, in their beauty of design, intricacy of function, and power to mediate love and service. It is to be 'at ease in our shape', that is, coming to terms with the body's imperfections – the parts that are weak, the parts that we feel are ugly, the parts that break easily and let us down.

It means coming to terms with one's psychological and emotional make-up. It means accepting one's intellectual and practical limitations as well as one's gifts, rejoicing in what has been given us rather than grieving over what has *not*; that only results in our becoming consumed with envy or paralysed by feelings of inferiority. It means developing one's potential rather than complaining of inadequacy. It means accepting the shape that has become 'us' through our past history – our childhood with its wounds and its influences, our adolescence and maturation. We need to see how far that shape is in process of transformation. What are the areas of flexibility, adaptability, change that will gradually alter our shape until Christ be formed in us and we take on more and more of his shape . . . or he fills ours?

Earthiness then, implies at-one-ness with passion, at-one-ness with our sexuality and at-one-ness with our shape.

It also implies an at-one-ness with the very earth itself and a reverent relationship to it.

We cannot celebrate our earthiness or glorify God in our bodies without the earth, and the work of ecologists today has reinforced for us more and more our fundamental and essential unity with Mother Earth. In this connection, Wendell Berry has said,

I have been groping for connections – that I think are

indissoluble, though obscured by modern ambitions –
between the spirit and the body, the body and other
bodies, the body and the earth ... It is impossible to
care for each other more or differently than we care for
the earth ... There is an uncanny resemblance between
our behaviour toward each other and our behaviour
toward the earth. Between our relation to our own sexuality and our relation to the reproductivity of the earth,
for instance.[15]

Along with a growing religious phenomenon known as
'New Age' thinking, which has been so influential in envi-
ronmentalist circles, has come a development in theological
insights into the relationship of God, humanity and the
whole creation, and the Church's role in 'healing the earth'.
Ever since environmentalism began growing in popularity
some twenty-five years ago, Christianity has been attacked
for its part in creating negative attitudes to the natural
world which have lain at the heart of the ecological crisis.
It has been argued by the critics (perhaps not entirely
fairly) that Christianity, with its teaching on the unre-
strained authority given to humanity over the earth, has
led to the attitude that, because ultimately the earth will
be destroyed, there is therefore little need to care for it.
They, too, have drawn attention to the false division Christianity has often made between spiritual realities and the
material world.

In a book entitled '*Tending the Garden*', one contributor,
Paulos Mar Gregorios, calls for an 'integral and particip-
ative' understanding of Christ. He claims that when Christ
assumed flesh, he took 'matter into himself' and he now
'shares his being with the whole created order: animals
and birds, snakes and worms, flowers and seeds'. Matter
is the creative energy of God in physical form. Thus, we
'should regard our human environment as the energy of
God in a form that is accessible to our senses'. In the light

of such an understanding, he asks, how do we view the world 'out there'?[16]

Far from heading for destruction, the earth is awaiting its redemption, eagerly longing to be set free from bondage and decay. Until such time it groans and travails – and so do we, for we are all caught up in the struggle that leads either to extinction or to transfiguration.

The Psalmist spoke of being 'a passing guest, as all our fathers were' (Ps. 39:12). He was referring to them as pilgrim people, of course, but we are only *guests* upon this good earth – very temporary ones. God is the gracious and abundant Host who has spread out in creation a banquet for our delight – a banquet that is there for our benefit, if we behave towards it as reverent guests. He has as Matthew Fox so rightly points out in *Original Blessing*, declared his banquet, in all its variety, to be 'very good' – including man himself whom he has formed out of earthiness but in his own image.

In hospitality, however, there are certain rules to be observed. Each culture has its own customs and traditions, and guests are required to act appropriately – responding with courtesy to the generosity of the host, and also observing the boundaries, not overstepping the mark or abusing that hospitality by taking liberties.

Today, in the face of the ecological crises of which we are being made increasingly aware, we have to acknowledge that humanity has lately been a bad guest on this earth. There is need for some severe discipline if we are to recover the art of respecting, savouring and thanking, which is what being a guest is all about. The hospitality of God requires an ever deepening reverence for all that is and all that might be[17] – for we are 'passing guests'. There will be others to follow who have an equal right to share the banquet – if we have left anything for them.

1. Louis Lavelle, *The Meaning of Holiness* (Burns and Oates 1951), pp. 1, 2.
2. Matthew Fox, Quoting Julian of Norwich in *Original Blessing* (Bear and Co. 1983), p. 63.
3. Annie Dillard, *Pilgrim at Tinker Creek* (New York 1975), p. 9, cited by Fox in *Original Blessing*, p. 42.
4. Stephen Verney, *Water into Wine* (Fount 1958), p. 180.
5. Hildegarde of Bingen; cited by Fox in *Original Blessing*, p. 57.
6. Ibid., p. 59.
7. Bishop Syresius, 'Lord Jesus, think on me', trans. A. W. Chatfield, *English Hymnal*, no. 77.
8. Lavelle, *The Meaning of Holiness*, p. 2.
9. Ibid., p. 2.
10. T. S. Eliot, 2nd Chorus from 'The Rock', *Collected Poems 1909–1962* (Faber 1963), p. 166.
11. Peter Dodson, *Contemplating the Word* (SPCK 1987), p. 35.
12. Margaret Evening, *Who Walk Alone* (Hodder 1974), p. 128.
13. Gilbert Russell, *Men and Women* (SCM 1948), pp. 15–16.
14. Charles Wesley, 'Jesu, Lover of my Soul', *English Hymnal*, no. 414.
15. Wendell Berry, cited by Fox in *Original Blessing*, p. 65.
16. *Tending the Garden: Essays on the Gospel and the Earth*, ed. W. G. Michaelson (Eerdmans 1987).
17. cf. Matthew Fox, *Original Blessing*, pp. 112–13.

2

The Door of Hope

The power of penitence

Soon afterwards he went on through cities and villages preaching and bringing good news of the Kingdom of God. And the twelve were with him and also some women who had been healed of evil spirits and infirmities: Mary, called Magdalen from whom seven demons had gone out . . . *(Luke 8:1–12)*

. . . her sins, her many sins must have been forgiven her, or she could not have shown such great love. It is the man who is forgiven little who shows little love *(Luke 7:49)*

So then, the very name, Mary Magdalen, conjures up a picture of an ardent, impulsive, passionate lover of the Lord who was prepared to throw all caution to the winds in her desire to show that love – whether it be by extravagant gift and gesture, or by courageously being with him in his sufferings to the end, or in her desire to be first at the tomb, close to the only part of her beloved Lord that she thought remained.

But another and equally strong strand in the tapestry of this woman's life is penitence. Clearly Mary's penitence is inextricably interwoven with her passionate love of the Lord. The words of Jesus in Luke 7:49 (see above), suggest that the depth of Mary's love was due to the extent of her forgiveness. But it is also true that penitence implies an existing relationship. It cannot stand in splendid isolation, unrelated to the one who has suffered because of the sin, but who has freely forgiven. The heart is stricken with sorrow when it realises how much it has grieved the one who is loved.

'Not only is it true that "We love because he first loved us" but we are enabled to make confession only and especially because he first loved us (1 John 4:19). The evidence of mercy and grace sparks in us a contrite heart . . .'[1]

Penitence is not only prompted by love, but also grows in response to love, for if we neither loved nor were loved we should hardly grieve if we were out of fellowship with the other. Sin separates us from God, sin puts us out of fellowship with him and with our fellow believers (whether they are aware of it or not). Sin is never a private affair. It affects the whole body of the Church. It is the desire to come home to the waiting Father whom we have so deeply injured and whose following love has been with us during our sojourn in the far country, patiently wooing us back, that brings us to the point of saying, 'I have sinned against heaven and before you and am no more worthy . . .' It is love of the brethren that brings us to the recognition that we need to be reconciled to them again.

Penitence is turning back to one whom we believe will receive us and delight to forgive us. Penitence brings a cleansing that opens up the channels for God's grace, mercy and healing power to flow to others. For this reason, it is an essential prerequisite of intercession. Penitence brings into harmony the disjointed bits of our life – even bringing physical wholeness where that disjointedness has caused muscular tension, headaches, arthritis, ulcers, heart trouble, etc. It is healthy to soul and body.

Penitence has all too often been associated with a dark and gloomy side of our Christian discipleship – somehow aligned with grovelling in abject sorrow, with the 'doing of penances' after scrupulous soul-baring, with '*Mea culpa*s' and much beating of the breast in a self-induced sense of unworthiness, with a very battered image of our self-worth – which may well be because we have never distinguished clearly enough in our own minds the essential difference between repentance and remorse. Repentance is creative whereas remorse is destructive. Peter repented of his denial and received forgiveness and a commission to more responsibility in his Master's service. It was a re-creation for him. Judas was filled with remorse and went out and hung himself. It was quite literally destructive. 'For godly grief produces a repentance that leads to salvation and brings no regret, but worldly grief produces death' (2 Cor. 7:10).

We need to realise that penitence is actually an essential prelude to the joy experienced, for example, by that great lover of the Lord, David (Ps. 51), by the Prodigal Son (Luke 15:24), by Peter (John 21) and of course by Mary Magdalen herself.

Basilea Schlink reminds us that:

> Long ago John the Baptist cried out, 'Repent, the Kingdom of Heaven is at hand.' Is that not the very basis of the Gospel, the Good News? Repentance – the gate to heaven! Repentance – the gate to the very heart of the Father! Yes, repentance makes us joyful and blissful. It brings us home to the heart of the Father; it brings us all the way to heaven.[2]

I was once told that Mother Basilea's Community of the Evangelical Sisterhood of Mary at Darmstadt used to begin its day with four hours of prayer, the first two of which were devoted to penitence (the second two hours to praise) – not of course entirely for the personal sin of each individual Sister, but for the corporate sin of all mankind in which we are involved and for which we must take our share of responsibility since we are part of humanity and bound up in the life of the world. Such comprehensive penitence is an extended way of praying the Agnus Dei: 'Lamb of God that takest away the sin of the world, have mercy on us.'

Penitence springs from sorrow: sorrow for the sin we ourselves have committed, grieving God and injuring our neighbour; sorrow for what we are – still falling so far short of the likeness of Christ; sorrow for our reluctance to grow. And also a shared sorrow for the world's Gadarene stampede towards self-destruction; sorrow for all the sordid mess of things, the corruption, the abuse of power, the destruction of natural resources, the vice, the collossal greed that divides mankind into the 'haves' and 'have nots', the lust, the violence and brutality, the unspeakably cruel devices that proceed, tragically, from that marvellous gift and image of God in man – the imagination; sorrow that the seeds of all this sin lie within ourselves. We have surely to acknowledge that given different circumstances of upbringing and environment they might even have flowered in us.

Much of sin is the misuse of good, and the misuse of this particular good (i.e. the imagination) has had more appalling consequences than perhaps any other. To take just one current example: the video 'Nasties' watched by vast numbers of people, including children, reveal depths of depravity and hideously vile sadism that would be beyond belief, were it not that there have been reports from reliable sources, especially those waging war against the production of such films. One is left sickened and gasping, totally at a loss as to how any human being could conceive and give birth to such unimaginable evil and cruelty. Where do the ideas come from? How do those responsible think them up in the first place? And why do they have such appeal to the voyeur in others?

With the entrance of sin into the world there came not only murder (Cain and Abel) but the actual pleasure of killing (Lamech, in Genesis). Man is the only species who *enjoys* killing for killing's sake, who can devise torture and watch his fellow beings die slowly and in agony. Animals may kill for food. The need to eat and provide for their young triggers off the hunting instinct. But, surely, the satisfaction is in the eating, not in the actual killing. Even where domesticated animals appear to play mercilessly with their prey, as a cat does with a mouse, when they no longer need to provide food for themselves, it is a response to a deep instinct only just below the surface in them, rather than calculated cruelty. It is to our peril that we forget what a power – 'divine and demonic – human imagination can be'. Speaking of what he calls the *Via Creativa*, Matthew Fox writes

> . . . it lays bare the immense demonic power that is coiled up in the very divine power, namely the imagination, of humanity. The divine and the demonic are very close together; only a thin line separates them/us. We who are indeed capable of divinity are also capable of the demonic. And the deepest of all demonic activity is the use of our divine imaginations to invent destruction.[3]

From these divine instruments have come the ovens of Auschwitz, the atom and napalm bombs, psychological and germ warfare, and now the means of nuclear warfare with its potential to bring global extinction.

When we pause to reflect on the enormity of the world's problem, as we must frequently do, perhaps we can understand the emphasis of the Darmstadt Sisters on repentance – not as a morbid, unhealthy scrupulosity about individual peccadilloes, but as those who 'stand in the gap' on behalf of the world's sin. As we come in this way as penitents, offering penitence for the world's sin, we come not just because we believe we *ought* to be sorry for the state of the world. We genuinely are. We long to be agents of reconciliation in the brokenness; agents of light in all the darkness; agents of love in the thick of hatred.

This sorrow is one of desperate pain – a redemptive pain. Blessed are those who bring cleansing to the world through their penitential tears. Blessed are those who mourn over the world and lament its sin, for they shall be comforted. And with the comfort comes a deep joy.

The experience of forgiveness is very akin to the experience of bereavement – so I have found. In both there is profound sorrow and a feeling of immense vulnerability. It is as though the top skin has been flicked off leaving raw flesh, exposed, unprotected and desperately tender to the touch. We feel terribly fragile. And yet there is a deep joy too. With forgiveness comes the joy of sharing in the heart of Christ as he weeps over the world, the joy of knowing that our prayers can be instrumental in the salvation of others, though we may never know just how, and the joy of knowing that we are reconciled not only to God but to our brothers in Christ. It is the same bond of fellowship and sense of support, the 'being in it together', suffering with, that gives rise to joy even in bereavement.

In both penitence and bereavement, we are surrounded and embraced by the love of God and of our fellow Christians even if we can't *feel* it. We know in our depths that unique experience of the comfort of God reserved for 'those who mourn', which is indeed blessed.

At its nub, penitence is a celebration. We celebrate the fact that the basic ingredients of our life are good; only our mishandling of them constitutes sin. Our use of the earth's resources may be sinful, the resources themselves are not. The use of our urges, passion, power to control may be sinful; the drive, the passion are not. The Psalmist knew this aspect of penitence from the inside when he said:

> O Lord my God, I cried to thee for help,
> And thou hast healed me . . .
> Weeping may tarry for the night,
> but joy comes with the morning . . .
> Thou hast turned for me my mourning into dancing;
> thou hast loosed my sackcloth
> and girded me with gladness,
> that my soul may praise thee and not be silent.
>
> (Ps. 30:2, 5, 11–12)

This must have been the experience of Mary Magdalen, too. The pouring of precious perfume in a costly act was a form of dancing, a dance of joy, of liberation and freedom from sin. 'Her sins, her many sins, must have been forgiven her, or she could not have shown such great love.' She had been loosed from sackcloth and girded with gladness and from henceforth her life was to be one of praise and adoration.

What the nature of the demons were which Jesus cast from her we don't know. We only know there was an overflowing gratitude that led to a life-long devotion. If she is to be identified with the woman 'with a bad name', presumably one of them could have been the demon of lust or the demon of despair at being on the receiving end of other's lust, for a prostitute can only be what she is if she has customers. She had probably been sinned against quite as much as she had sinned. Like many other women of her day, and since, she may have had no other means of financial support.

Clearly the fact that this information about her is recorded by Luke, years after the event, means that people had not forgotten her past. The memory of this remarkable conversion remained for them and obviously for her. Her sins were forgiven but not necessarily obliterated from her memory.

What do we actually *do* with painful memories from the past? Maybe we try and bury them – they are 'forgotten and gone', we say. But they are neither. All memories are stored away – never gone. It is only our power of recall which is selective and may diminish in certain respects with age or illness. But all our memories impinge upon our present living, whether we realise it or not. The good memories quietly feed into us a sense of well-being, security and confidence in the goodness of life. They free us to grow and move forward in our journey. For example, the baby who takes into life good memories of birthing and bonding is likely to be secure in a way that a child with traumatic memories of both is not.

The unhealed memories are sometimes screaming away even in the unconscious, clamouring for attention and sapping our energies, as long as they are ignored. They undermine our sense of self-worth, trap us in fear, keep alive guilt feelings. They make us unfree to respond with joy to the opportunities and demands of the present.

Albert Camus tells the story, in *La Chute*, of a young lawyer in Paris, who, one night, as he was walking alongside a river, heard a woman's scream from a nearby bridge, a splash and then further cries of distress. He chose to ignore them and walked on. In the papers next day he read that a young woman's body had been dragged out of the Seine. The years passed and the memory haunted him – constantly, doggedly – until one day, in desperation, he cried out: 'Young woman, throw yourself into the river again that I may save both of us.' He discovered, as we all must, that we are not saved by forgetting or cancelling our memory of concrete guilt'.[4]

Rarely a day goes by without our reading in the papers, or seeing on TV, the news of an appalling natural disaster, a terrible accident or a tragedy in which people actually see loved ones killed before their eyes. How do those involved in such traumatic events ever cope with the memories? Many go on reliving the incident in nightmares. Dreams carry their own power to heal. Some may be fortunate enough to meet a person and/or group that can lead them gently back into the hurt areas and expose them for healing, helping them to find God even in the midst of so much tragedy and suffering.

What is true of individual needs in this respect is true of groups. There is much need throughout the world today for the healing of collective memories – in Northern Ireland, in South Africa, in the Middle East, in Cambodia, El Salvador, Guatamala, between East and West.

At the 1986 Assembly of the Baptist World Alliance held in Germany, for the first time since World War II, the leaders of the West German delegation hosting the conference stood before the Assembly and asked for forgiveness of the other member countries of the Alliance for the atrocities committed by the Nazis especially against the Jews. They confessed the need of healing of a national memory – even though many of them as individuals had not yet been born at the time of the Holocaust.

Confession and healing are the only answer for painful memories; forgetting is not. Unless we are to be crippled by our past failures, by the reproach and shame they bring, we need a real conversion of memories. Mary Magdalen was set free by such a conversion.

I distinguish between healing and conversion, though ideally they go together, in the sense that with healing, the sting of the memory is removed, its power to plunge people into self-hate is destroyed. But, with conversion, *the memory is transfigured* into a positive good. It becomes a tool which we can use in the service of others in *their* growth towards healing and wholeness. The memory can be there at our command, endlessly to be retrieved and revived as a source of energy. 'Salvation does not bypass the history and memory of guilt, but rather builds upon and from it'.[5] The very place of failure becomes the place of strength because it is there that we have been forced to acknowledge our weakness, there that we have grown in humility and dependence upon God.

For Israel, the wilderness was a place crammed full with memories. Amongst them were the many memories of disobedience and failure – the grumbling, the putting God to the test, the idolatry, the unbelief and lack of trust, the murmuring, the moaning, the hankering after the fleshpots of Egypt and hence the bondage which, they seemed to forget, went with them.

Through his wife's treachery and infidelity, Hosea was given insight into something of what Israel's disobedience and unfaithfulness meant to God – how God's heart was broken just as his own had been broken over Gomer's adultery. He felt the pain God must have felt when his people 'whored after other gods'. Yet, he speaks of God wooing his people back after their infidelity, alluring them into the wilderness to speak tenderly to them; taking them back in remembrance to the place of their youth (as a nation) their first commitment, their bridal oath, his covenant-making with them.

> Therefore, behold I will allure her,
> and bring her into the wilderness,
> and speak tenderly to her.
> And there I will give her her vineyards,
> and make the Valley of Achor a door of hope.
> And there she shall answer as in the days of her youth,
> as at the time when she came out of Egypt . . .
> And I will betroth you to me for ever; I will betroth you
> to me in righteousness and in justice, in steadfast love,
> and in mercy. I will betroth you to me in faithfulness;
> and you shall know the Lord.
>
> (Hos. 2:14–15, 19)

God takes them back in memory to that part of their history that was fraught with failures but from which they emerged a nation forged, as it were, in the crucible of fire that the wilderness undoubtedly was (physically and spiritually). In their renewed failure, he causes them to recall the place of original weakness.

For many of us, these have been significant verses in retreat as we have gone into the wilderness to allow the Lord to speak tenderly to us, to restore and revitalise our relationship with him, to heal our backsliding and failure to live out the radical commitment to him that we vowed at baptism, ordination, profession, etc., to heal our many disobediences, our 'going it alone' in our own strength.

In the desert of our retreat *we* may long to renew *our* commitment to him. On his part, *he* yearns to make us fruitful – the vineyards in the midst of barrenness, of which Hosea speaks.

We may, however, have stopped short there and not allowed the next verse to yield its full glory: 'And I will make the Valley of Achor the door of hope' (Hos. 2:15). The Valley of Achor stood for the Israelites as a perpetual and accursed reminder of an occasion of disobedience. At the battle of Ai, the Israelites had been defeated by the Amorites – not just defeated, they had actually turned tail and fled before the enemy. The ignominy and shame were more than they could bear. What had happened to the Lord, the Victorious One, who was supposed to be on their side and had in the past conquests proved a mighty warrior of power? What would happen to their reputation among the other nations? Would they become a laughing stock? Were they not the people whom other nations always feared for the Lord was with them? Were they not known as the God-with-us people? Why had he deserted them at this hour? Who or what had displeased him? Someone must have sinned and that someone would have to be found.

We know how an interrogation procedure took place whereby tribe by tribe was questioned, then family by family and household by household, until finally (seeing the elimination process left him no escape) Achan confessed his sin (Josh. 7:20–1) He had kept back some of the booty from the previous battle, taken some of the 'devoted things' and hidden them in his tent. He had been disobedient. He had taken back that which had been vowed to God (. . . and which of us hasn't at some time or other?). Yet as one Hindu-Christian writer put it, 'There can be no taking back when something has been truly given.'[6]

So serious a view did the Israelites take of this sin, that Joshua had no choice but to condemn Achan and his entire household to execution – the children and servants included, his flocks, his cattle, his goods and chattels . . . *anything* that could have suffered the contamination of sin by proximity to Achan, all who were bound up in the corporate personality of the family and therefore the corporate responsibility.

All were slaughtered – first by stoning, then burning, in the Valley of Achor. After which, the Valley of Achor became a place of bitter, accursed memories, a reminder of shameful defect.

This then is the place that Hosea sees as the symbol of Israel's disobedience – Israel who has taken back her first love, her loyalty and devotion and bestowed her favours on other gods. Yet this is the very place that will become the door of hope.

We all of us have our own Valley of Achor – just as Jacob the deceiver had his, Moses the murderer had his, David the adulterer his, Peter the denier his, the Apostles the deserters theirs, Paul the persecutor his and of course Mary Magdalen the woman 'with a bad name' hers. And further on in the history of the Church, we see the saints emerging from their Valleys of Achor – Augustine, Francis of Assisi, Ignatius Loyola, Ramon Lull, Charles de Foucauld, Thomas Merton – all men who had led at some point wild and profligate lives.

For most of these people, their Valley had to do with the wrong use of passion. But for many the door of hope was opened when it became *converted* passion. It was the very power of that passion which set them ablaze with love for God, with a missionary fervour which filled them with a zeal that would brook no compromise.

It is an awesome thing, as Paul knew, to experience forgiveness and the healing and conversion of memories – and then to find the very ground of our weakness becoming the place of strength (2 Cor. 12:7–9), our wounds becoming stars, as Mother Julian put it, in her *Revelations of Divine Love*, the thickened scar tissue becoming stronger than the original, undamaged flesh, the healed failure or forgiven disobedience being the place where Christ's power rests upon us like a tent pitched over our very weakness (2 Cor. 12:9), blessedly leading to poverty of spirit. We end up with a plus quality in God's service.

Though healed, the soul's wounds are still seen by God, not as wounds, but as honourable scars . . . For in his lovers he regards sin as a sorrow and a suffering, and, because of his love, not as blameworthy . . . Our cour-

teous Lord does not want his servants to despair, even
if they fall frequently and grievously. Our falling does
not stop his loving us.[7]

He takes the place of shame and transfigures it into the
place of glory.

To the question, 'Are we to sin, fail, descend into the
Valley of Achor that grace may abound?' we would
certainly want to respond with St Paul, 'God forbid!' Yet
which of us has not known the bitter-sweet experience of
coming home to the Father, the tenderness described by
Hosea in his final chapter?

> Return, O Israel to the Lord your God,
> for you have stumbled because of your iniquity . . .
> I will heal their faithlessness;
> I will love them freely,
> for my anger has turned from them . . .
> They shall return and dwell beneath my shadow,
> they shall flourish as a garden;
> they shall blossom as a vine,
> their fragrance shall be like the wine of Lebanon.
>
> (Hos. 14:1, 4, 7)

The Valley of Achor has been for us a door of hope, a
place of fruitfulness as indeed Isaiah saw it becoming, quite
literally, for Israel (Isa. 65:10).

We do not sin that grace may abound, but, incredibly,
in the face of our sinning, grace goes on abounding. For
probably we have not one Valley of Achor in our lives, but
a succession.

They can of course, if we choose to ignore them, remain
places split off from our conscious memories, places
accursed in our experience – too awful and too shameful
even to return to them consciously and deliberately but, in
consequence therefore, areas in which we remain cut off
from God. Part of the work of healing and forgiveness is
to walk back into the Valley of Achor taking Jesus with

us, so that his saving presence can redeem the accursed place and heal the memory. But, even more, so that through a renewing of covenant love, he can transfigure that valley into a gateway of hope, for in remembering we are re-membered, put together and made whole.

On one occasion when I was staying at Lee Abbey in north Devon, I looked out of the bedroom window early one morning and saw that the fields leading down to Lee Bay were still in darkness. But just a touch of light was beginning to pick out the craggy headlands so that they stood silhouetted against the sky. Suddenly the sun rose over the hill behind the house and shone directly down on to a white gate just below my window. The strength of the sun made the gate a dazzling, brilliant white. It picked it out so that it was an immediate focus of attention in a scene where all else was in shadow. And the words of this verse came to mind – the darkness, the Valley of Achor, will become a door of hope.

A few minutes later, I went back to the window, and now the sun, even brighter, had picked out a second gate leading into a further field down the hill, then a third and a fourth and fifth – a whole succession of white gates stretching ahead, leading from one field to another right down to the sea.

Not one valley but many. Not one door of hope but a succession of doors. Not one experience of mercy but a continuing one, for:

> The steadfast love of the Lord never ceases,
> his mercies never come to an end;
> they are new every morning;
> great is thy faithfulness.

(Lam. 3:22–3)

1. Richard Foster, *Celebration of Discipline* (Hodder 1980), p. 132.

2. Basilea Schlink, *Repentance: the Joy-filled Life* (Lakeland 1969), p. 13.
3. Matthew Fox, *Original Blessing*, (Bear and Co, 1983), p. 232.
4. Rowan Williams, *Resurrection* (Darton Longman and Todd 1982), p. 12.
5. Ibid, p. 12.
6. Abhishiktananda, *Guru and Disciple* (SPCK 1974), p. 57.
7. Julian of Norwich, *Revelations of Divine Love*, trans. Clifton Wolters (Penguin 1966), ch. 39, p. 121.

Crazed with Love

The power of fervour

To my bare feet, Lord
through the surging grass,
grant a clean, long stride
as to you I race.
           (Marie-Noel)[1]

Wisdom 'tis and courtesy
Crazed for Jesus to be.
           (Laude LXXXIV)[2]

All the world loves a lover. Whatever gaps we may have
in our knowledge of Mary Magdalen, her love for Jesus is
indisputable. As we have seen, she could not have shown
such love had she not been so greatly forgiven (Luke 7:47).
She could not have shown such love had she been afraid
to love, inhibited and unable to express it. She could not
have shown it had she feared *being* loved.

> Just as I am, Thy love unknown
> Has broken every barrier down.[3]

That's the trouble! Love breaks down barriers. And since
it is an unknown quantity, a limitless flow of power, many
fear it – unless it can be controlled, contained, made
predictable, manageable, something we can handle without
finding our defences gone. 'Most people are deeply frightened of unconditional love and its power to expand the
freedom of the loved one. They therefore want to institu-
tionalize it, regulate it, surround it with restrictions,
conventions – anything to make it safe.'[4]

That is precisely what the onlookers sought to do when Mary brought her alabaster flask of costly perfume to anoint Jesus. They took refuge in propriety. 'This unconventional behaviour is out of hand. Jesus should put a stop to it, or get it in control.' It is touching off deep fears, too powerful to tolerate.

They can give as the reason for their strong reaction words like 'embarrassing', 'distasteful', but they can't actually articulate what lies at the heart of their fear. They are only aware of a desperate need for restraint. And so they resort to historical facts. They drag up the past. 'If he knew what sort of woman this was, he wouldn't allow her to be so close to him, touching him, weeping over him, assuming a personal relationship.' They are apparently unaware of the *immediate* past. They know nothing of the 'many sins *which have been forgiven*'. They are obviously not *that* concerned about the woman's welfare since they don't even know of her *metanoia*, her conversion. (How often the lingering memories of a person's *past* failings prevent us from seeing how they have grown through love, and how the grace of God has worked a change in them. We ignore the reality of sanctification which is dynamic, never static.)

Then, they turn to a theological argument. 'If this man were a prophet . . . he would have greater insight into her character and behave more fittingly for a prophet,' as though they believed that it was laid down, somewhere, that a prophet should keep a proper distance from sinners, and safeguard his integrity at the expense of compassion and love. Yet, the true prophetic stance is one of identification and co-inherence with mankind: hence Jesus came to John for baptism in the Jordan; Isaiah acknowledged that he was a 'man of unclean lips who dwelt in the midst of a people of unclean lips'. The greater the purity of the prophet, the greater was his capacity for compassion. The misunderstanding of these critics of both the prophet and Jesus was tragic.

Next they present a financial objection. This woman has

been responsible for a colossal loss – in monetary terms. For this perfume in its alabaster jar could have fetched an exceedingly high price on the market. 'To what purpose is this waste?' they cry in indignation. 'What right has she to indulge in this extravagance in the face of so much poverty?' Now comes the social concern! 'The perfume could have been sold and the money given to the poor,' they claim. Is this concern for the poor consistent in their lives, or is it brought in at this point simply to strengthen their case, to fuel their opposition? To what? An outrageous and extravagant act on the part of a woman? Indeed. But far more. It is the love, extravagantly, foolishly, outrageously displayed that terrifies them. They simply can't cope with the *depth* of this woman's love; hence objections are conjured up from as many angles as possible.

The world has never been able to cope with *depth* in people's love for Christ. Jesus warned his followers of this. He was totally honest with them when he told them that they would be persecuted, stoned, rejected, hounded from place to place, accused falsely, slandered and reviled, put to death 'for my sake and the Gospel's'. The more ardent the love the more certain persecution will be. In our day, when compromise and moderation are the norm and ardour and burning zeal rather more unusual, it is easy to forget the depth of love for Christ shown by some of the early Christians, the penalties for which were terrible beyond description. We all know about the arenas and the lions, the burnings at the stake, the beheadings . . . but, relatively speaking, these were fairly merciful deaths. Others were wrapped in pitch, set alight and used as living torches to provide flood lights for Nero's garden parties. Some were sewn in the skins of wild animals before the Emperor's hunting dogs were set upon them to tear them limb from limb. There was the rack. Molten lead was poured upon them, red hot plates applied to the most tender areas of the body, they were mutilated, parts of their body torn out or hacked off and roasted before their eyes, they were burned whilst cold water was poured over the affected parts to increase and lengthen the agony.

We are familiar with some equally brutal forms of torture in our own day and age, usually meted out to political prisoners, with the addition now of more sophisticated types of torture applied in the psychiatric wards. Often torture today is inflicted as punishment for loyalty to a political cause, a loyalty that can end in fanaticism. In part, of course, the Roman persecution was a political affair. Christians who refused to burn a pinch of incense to the godhead Caesar and say, 'Caesar is Lord', were enemies of the State. Compromise would have been so easy. Some of course took that way. They fell prey to the same temptation that Jesus faced in the wilderness, and subsequently in his ministry, when he was persuaded (by Satan, or Peter acting as a mouthpiece for Satan) 'You don't have to suffer. If you take the way of compromise you can avoid the inevitable clash and the suffering it will bring.'

Caesar-worship was primarily a test of political loyalty. As it happened, when a man had burned his pinch of incense to Caesar he was given a certificate to prove his loyalty, and he could then go away and worship any god he liked provided he didn't disturb the peace or become a public nuisance. But the Christians refused a double standard. They wouldn't take the easier path of compromise. When confronted with the choice of 'Caesar or Christ', it could only be Christ. Their acclamation of faith was 'Jesus is Lord', and they would give that title to no other. So a Christian was automatically outlawed by his firm stand for his Lord. The strength of the Roman Empire lay in its unity and it could not afford pockets of disloyalty. The Christians suffered the consequences.

The reason for the persecution may well have been chiefly political, but from the Christian's point of view it was a loyalty of deep and fierce devotion to Jesus, and thousands of them demonstrated the extravagance of love.

The late Dr Martin Niemöller once claimed that persecution should be the norm of the Church. Any Church not facing persecution was subnormal. He spoke, of course, against the background of Nazi oppression and his own stand against it within the German Confessional Church. And for that stand, he himself spent four years in solitary confinement. We can see the point he was making. A Church on fire with love for Christ, individual Christians full of burning zeal, will never be simply tolerated or go unnoticed. They 'turn the world upside down' (Acts 17:6) wherever they happen to be. They challenge mediocrity and half-heartedness. Their all-or-nothingness for the Gospel polarises standards; there are blacks and whites, but few grey areas for them. They can even seem harsh in the extremes of their wholeheartedness. But for them, 'he that is not for Jesus is against him' (cf. Matt. 12:30). They are either welcomed gladly or hated and persecuted.

The ardour and burning zeal of some of the early saints sometimes led to what was described as 'holy madness'. Such was the intensity of their devotion to Christ, the world wrote them off as 'holy simpletons' crazy with love. They watched them renounce their wealth, leave their homes and material security, and go out into the desert to a life of dedication, prayer and physical hardship. They observed others giving themselves in service to the outcast, the poor, the untouchables – kissing lepers' wounds, sharing their homes and food with those infected with deadly diseases. They noted the unflagging zeal of those who wandered the earth, without material support, often facing enormous physical hazards, fatigue and sickness, in order to preach the Gospel.

The 'holy simpletons' themselves often regarded discretion as the enemy of true devotion. Their life had 'a tang, a salt-sting' which ours often lacks.[5] They succeeded where a broader, saner, more cautious and prudent way of life fails. No half-measures, no cowardice or compromise – that was their approach to life.

In the world today, some of those who never darken the door of a church nevertheless read St John of the Cross, Walter Hilton, St Francis, St Thérèse, de Caussade, Merton. I once had an intriguing discussion with two young people (in the days of Hippies) who nobbled me at Victoria Coach Station and seemed anxious to question me about methods of meditation. They produced from the hip pockets of their faded jeans, well thumbed paper-back copies of de Caussade's *Self Abandonment to Divine Providence* and *The Cloud of Unknowing*.

As E. Herman wrote,

> While we strain our ingenuity and the inclusive power of Christianity to the utmost in our efforts to win these gifted young people of a decadent civilisation, they receive with grateful hearts a grain of true leaven, a spark of the hidden fire, from the fleshless hands of these forbidding [holy madmen].[6]

The extravagance of love is the very stuff of God himself, who has shown the utmost extravagance in creation, in Covenant love, in redemptive suffering, in salvation and transfiguration. Whatever we may feel about the way ascetics of earlier days despised the world and neglected their bodies, turned away from simple joy in natural beauty and the marvels of animal life, denied natural instincts and subjected the body to harsh punishments in their pursuit of holiness, nevertheless, in their day they 'turned the world upside down'.

> Their minds were turned to another key. Their only wisdom was to keep their souls fixed on their Lord with the directness and simplicity of loving intention, meeting every demand, evading nothing, questioning nothing. They called him Beloved, and fastened his name on their hearts not in a weakly, sentimental mood, but in fixed and unalterable purpose, pledging themselves in simple fidelity and courage to do and dare, to suffer and endure

all he bids them, all his service involves. Inspired by so
deep and enabling a passion their way of life was
redeemed from the selfishness and pettiness that could
sometimes be found in ascetics. 'They suffered not to
gain salvation for their own souls, but with Christ; and
with Christ, for the Church and for the world.'[7]

The words of Richard Rolle describe fairly accurately
the place at which Mary Magdalen was when she came to
pour out her perfume, her tears and her love upon Jesus.
Hers was 'love without measure, desire without limit,
longing without order and burning without discretion'.[8]

For Mary's critics, it was not only the 'love without
measure' that triggered off so much fear, but the feminine
way of expressing it. It was not by any means the only
time feminine expressions of piety have been frowned upon,
whether found in women or men.

On one occasion a group of us in Oxford attending a
Spirituality Workshop were invited to engage in some role
play. Divided into groups of three, one member was asked
to play Jesus, one Simon (or one of the critics), one Mary
Magdalen. In our group the dialogue got off to an
aggressive start when Simon rounded fiercely on Jesus and
used some very forceful language to express his anger,
disgust and (although he would not admit it) his fear at
the episode he had just witnessed. Why hadn't Jesus
checked Mary? Why did he encourage these women and
the publicans and sinners to hang round him? Why did he
seem to enjoy the attention this woman gave him at the
expense of decency, propriety and consideration for the
feelings of the men present? Why did he allow this abuse
of hospitality? – and so on. The accusations were sharp
and bitterly expressed. In reply, Jesus had some equally
fierce rebukes to administer. He was stern in his criticism,
righteously angry, eloquent in his attempt to explain his
attitude and in reasoning with Simon. Meanwhile, Mary
could not get a word in. Finally, she burst forth. Indeed,

she blazed as she challenged Simon's suggestion that she
was attention-seeking; his implication that she had designs
on Jesus (as he had reminded her she had in the past had
on other men); his claim that this display of emotion was
unseemly, unattractive, embarrassing and totally out of
place. She had no right to be there anyway without invitation, he had said. The guest list had been entirely a male
one.

'All right!' she said, 'Let me tell you how it feels to be
a woman in this situation. You men can approach Jesus
without impediment, whenever you like. There are no rules
to say that this is 'not done'. Those who love him, such as
his disciples, are free to be with him night and day. They
enjoy his company, sit at his feet, drink in his words, watch
him at prayer, accompany him on his travels, witness his
miracles, act as his agents, share in some of his most
intimate moments with the Father. They are able to put
questions to him, listen to his teaching, ask for interpretation of his parables, share his joys as well as his hardships
– maybe even bask in his reflected glory. Apart from the
times when he seeks solitude, they have him the whole
time.

'But when can a woman get near to him to enjoy his
company? A haemorrhaging woman dare only sneak up
from behind and touch the hem of his garment. Even then
it is difficult to edge close enough to find a space between
his bodyguard of disciples. He loves little children. But
when women bring them to be touched and held and
blessed by Jesus, the disciples block the way (or try to).
When he is found sitting by a well talking to a woman,
alone, the disciples are clearly shocked. A woman's life can
be totally changed by an encounter with Jesus, but from
then on she is expected to keep a respectable distance from
him.

'Women may love him with a burning devotion, but
what avenues are open to them for showing it?

'Oh yes, a group of us have been following the Lord

and his disciples ever since they left Galilee, but always discreetly in the background. Yet we need *him* and he appreciates *us*. Why else does he choose the company of Martha and Mary of Bethany for relaxation?

'Don't you understand my crying need? Yes, literally *crying* need! What is so embarrassing about that? Why can't you men cope with tears or understand their language? Don't you realise what I was saying by them?

'And the gesture, the pouring out of ointment at great expense? What did that really matter to you? Why were you so uptight? Do you not understand anointing and its implications?

'If you want the truth, this was a baptism of love. I longed that he might baptise me, but that was not appropriate for he didn't baptise people himself. Yet I knew that I was bound to him in bonds of covenant love for life. So I decided to reverse the act and baptise *him*, in the water of my tears; to pour oil over his head, to show by this act that I renounced evil, that I turned to him, that I believed and trusted in him; to show him that I intended to make a life-long commitment to him; to assure him that I would suffer with him, die with him if need be, and follow him till my life's end.

'Love *has* to be expressed. You cannot dam it up by conventions and rules. I don't care how people interpreted my act and what insinuations they chose to make. He understood and that is all that matters. *He* accepted the expression of my love as a pure thing. He saw the heart that longed to be united to him. He interpreted my tears as sacramental and the anointing as symbolic. He saw me not as a prostitute but as a priest.'

This, remember, was a spontaneous bit of role play not a well thought out speech, or prepared dialogue. None of us at that workshop had come prepared for this imaginative exercise. However fanciful it may seem (and I have reproduced it as accurately as I could, knowing that it is open to all sorts of criticism), perhaps it points up some of the sheer frustration a woman like Mary Magdalen must have felt. And doubtless there were others, beside her, who do not feature by name in the gospels but who were filled with undying gratitude and love. Would Jairus's daughter have wanted to meet Jesus again and get to know better the man who had recalled her so gently from that journey into the next life? The mothers of those healed, of babies blessed, the sisters of the disciples, the women in whose homes the travelling band received hospitality – did they never long to have the opportunity of a one-to-one conversation and more intimate sharing? Did they never ache for the chance of a personal encounter and his undivided attention – just for a few moments?

Obviously the cultural differences of that generation did not encourage such expectations, as ours might. But nevertheless, a woman's need was there, even if repressed. It is still there. Could it account for the predominance of women in the Church, the far greater number of women religious than men? And yet, in leadership, the Church is still male-dominated; women's ministry accepted only with caution and certain misgivings by some.*

There are four accounts of the story of the woman who anointed Jesus. In most people's minds, she is remembered as a sinner, someone with a 'bad name' whose grave sins have been forgiven. Hence the strong tradition that associates Mary Magdalen with this act. But, in actual fact, it is only in Luke's account (Luke 7:36–50) that any mention is made of the woman being a sinner.

In Matthew and Mark (Matt. 26:6–13; Mark 14:3–9) the event takes place in the house of Simon the leper at Bethany. John's account (John 12:1–8) also places it at Bethany, but in the house of Mary and Martha. (Perhaps this is the reason why some have been led to identify Mary of Bethany with the converted Mary Magdalen). Out of

---

* This is not a reference to the Movement for the *Ordination* of Women in particular, but a more general comment on women's *ministry*.

the four accounts, three of them speak of this act as a preparation for burial.

Matthew: 'she poured this ointment on my body . . . to prepare me for burial . . .'

Mark: 'She has anointed my body beforehand for its burial.'

John: 'She had to keep this scent for the day of my burial . . .'

In John's version, the raising of Lazarus is mentioned and Lazarus is said to be present at the meal, Martha serving. Mary's generosity and extravagance in bringing in the pure nard and anointing the *feet* of Jesus, could have been seen as an act of overwhelming gratitude for the return of her brother.

In Matthew and Mark's accounts, the woman anoints the *head* of Jesus. The expression 'to anoint one's head with oil' is a gesture of hospitality in the East – a gesture which had been conspicuously absent in Simon's hosting. But it held a much deeper meaning and significance too.

To anoint was a priestly or prophetic task. Samuel anointed Saul and David. The King was the Lord's 'Anointed One'. Baptism for Jesus was an anointing as Messiah King as well as ordination to be Suffering Servant.

Here, the woman fulfils a prophetic role. Six days before the Passover, she carries out a prophetic act, not only in recognition of Christ's kingship but as a symbolic warning as to where it is leading. The disciples had attempted to dissuade Jesus from going up to Jerusalem. He had gone nevertheless. Now a woman speaks to him, in powerful symbol, of his forthcoming death if he pursues his present course. He understands the warning she is giving even though he chooses to ignore it. His disciples couldn't see further than the 300 denarii the perfume could have fetched, had it been sold. They lacked the intuitive power of this woman, lacked the sensitivity to the danger he was in.

In two versions of the story, the woman is a priest, in

three of them she is a prophet, in only one of them is she referred to as a sinner. In Luke's Gospel, the date of the incident is changed, the role is changed; the dinner party takes place earlier in Christ's ministry, she is not prophet or priest but prostitute. Strangely, that last is the image people seem to fasten upon most readily. I wonder why? And what that is saying about our attitude to women, even today?[9]

In the Upper Room, Jesus broke bread and poured out wine – symbols of his body and blood – and enjoined his disciples to continue to do this 'in remembrance of me'.

At the end of this pre-anointing before burial he says that wherever the Good News is proclaimed what the woman has done will be told 'in remembrance of her'. The 'remembering' would reactivate the same love and devotion in succeeding generations of those who heard of her act of reckless love.

For, despite the difference in these versions, one thing stands out in common. This *was* an act of love – unashamed, fearless love; love that was so great it could be shown in public, disregarding what people might think or say; love that could show emotion; that contained deeply intuitive understanding and sensitive concern. It was love that had to be expressed in action – even extravagant action. It was love that flowed freely as did the tears; was poured out as generously as was the ointment. It was love that was 'a passionate affair of the heart, the energy of which could transform a human relationship and make it the very stuff of the Kingdom'.[10]

There may be times in our lives when we love unwisely, but nevertheless we learn by such love. There are times when we may express it inappropriately or curb its expression too severely. We learn by this too. There is no crime in making mistakes in our loving – only in not loving at all. If this is true in human relationships, how much more in our relationship with Jesus who loves us so much, we can only be 'crazed with love' in return.

Ramon Lull tells this story,

The Lover went to seek his Beloved, and he found a man who was dying without love. And he said: 'How great a sadness is it that any man should die without love!' So the Lover said to him that was dying: 'Say, why dost thou die without love?' And he replied: 'Because I lived without love.'[11]

1. Marie-Noel, cited in *The Hermitage Within* by a Cistercian Monk (Darton Longman and Todd 1977), p. 100.
2. Jacopone da Todi, Underhill, *Laude* (Dent 1919), p. 283.
3. Charlotte Elliott (1789–1871), 'Just as I am without one plea', *English Hymnal*, no. 316.
4. Charles Elliott, *Praying the Kingdom* (Darton, Longman and Todd 1985), p. 64.
5. E. Herman, *The Meaning and Value of Mysticism* (James Clarke, 1915), p. 177.
6. Ibid.
7. Ibid.
8. Richard Rolle, *Fire of Love* (Penguin 1972), ch. 17.
9. I am indebted to Sister Margaret Kelly OP for a paper (given at Nazareth House, Pretoria, April 1987) in which she pointed out the distinctions of prophet, priest and prostitute.
10. Adapted from Elliott, *Praying the Kingdom*, p. 79.
11. Ramon Lull, *The Book of The Lover and The Beloved*, 84, cited in *A Dazzling Darkness*, ed. Patrick Grant (Fount 1985), p. 147–8.

4

Losing is Finding

The power in darkness

I sought him whom my soul loves;
I sought him, but found him not;
I called him, but he gave no answer. . . .
'I will seek him whom my soul loves.'
I sought him but found him not. . . .
'Have you seen him whom my soul loves?'
(Song of Solomon 3:1–3)

Here you are, in tears, outside a tomb.
But my tomb is your heart, and there I am not
dead, but resting, and alive for all eternity.
Your soul is my garden, and you are right to
suppose that I am the gardener. I am the new
Adam, and I both care for my paradise and protect it.
(Anonymous, 13th century)

Jesus is dead. She still cannot grasp it. Her whole life has revolved around him ever since her healing and absolution. She has followed him both close to and from afar. One amongst the 'women who followed him from Galilee', (Luke 23:55) she has tried to be useful to the group of disciples – maybe arranging accommodation in their wanderings, acquiring supplies of food, going ahead to arrange for or prepare meals. One wonders if these women, who followed them to minister to their needs, dealt with their laundry and mending? Perhaps tended them in sickness? We can only conjecture. But the Gospels make it quite explicit that they were there in the background and it must surely have been for a purpose. The last week in

Jerusalem had been a harrowing one. Each day the menace of a climactic confrontation with the religious authorities loomed larger, the threatening clouds grew darker. She watched her Lord's suffering deepen, well before the final crisis of trial and execution. And this brought out in her a feverish activity – a 'being there' with him minute by minute, in spirit even when she could not be physically near him.

It is important to recognise that in the face of suffering women need to go into action. To acknowledge this helps us to accept the very different reactions of men and women in certain situations.

In his book, *Praying the Kingdom*, Charles Elliott cites the experience of a religious sister who specialises in spiritual direction.

> She often gives aspirants the exercise of imaginatively attending the scene of the crucifixion. She encourages them to enter deeply into that moment of history; to imagine the sounds, the smells, the light, the feel, the atmosphere; to look deeply into the faces of people standing round the cross; to watch and particularly listen to the Lord, as, struggling for breath, he heaves himself into a more erect position on the cross, defying the pain in his feet and wrists, to gain a lungful of air . . . 'Now' the sister says, 'you are there: what do you do?' . . . and, she reports, 'the extraordinary thing is, almost without exception, men can't take it. They go away. They simply can't stand watching that intensity of suffering. So they slope off. Women can't stand it, either. But they are determined to save him. So they fling themselves at the cross to cut him free. Or they start rallying the crowds to take on the Roman soldiers. The one thing they can't manage in the face of such evident wretchedness is inactivity.[1]

(The one notable exception to that in the original situation was Mary, the mother of Jesus.)

So, Mary Magdalen has been caught up in a whirl of activity, an activity that is both her response to and her need in the face of Jesus' sufferings. Then the actual trial and death had been a nightmare – did she perhaps act as a messenger, flying from house to house? Was she running around seeking out the place where Jesus was being tried, following him doggedly in the hope of a glimpse, a small opportunity to do something for him in these dark hours? And then came the crucifixion itself – hideous in the extreme, unbearable to watch, and yet she was compelled by love to be there, to look upon the suffering of her loved one, to enter into it with him, to be near him in loving support, easing a little of his pain by accompanying his mother, offering to her daughterly concern.

And finally the last agony and the last moments of his earthly life, the dying words, the bowing of his head and the yielding of his spirit. Darkness over the earth. The end.

Not quite! There are things still to do – the body to be removed from the cross and transferred to the garden of Joseph Arimathea. She and other of the women accompany the body, sit over against the sepulchre and watch the sealing of the tomb. There was the rush to complete the preliminary washing of the body in the short while before sunset when the stone would be rolled in front of the tomb. The more elaborate rituals would have to wait until after the Sabbath. Then . . .?? Home? To Mary's house? To Mary the mother of John Mark? We don't know where she and the other women stayed during those hours between sundown on Friday and dawn on that 'first day of the week'.

We can begin to imagine the grief and sense of loss. But always there was something more to do. Isn't it very often the numerous things that have to be done after a death that help people through the initial stages of bereavement? The registering of the death and obtaining a certificate, the funeral arrangements with undertaker and priest, the moving of the body, the notifying of relatives, the clearing of belongings. These all help to stave off the awful moment of emptiness. There is the funeral to 'look forward to' – not necessarily with joyful anticipation, but there is still a body, there is still a physical focus of attention on the loved one. The family gather, they draw on happy memories and share them, everyone wants to think well of the loved one even if there have been difficulties in relationship during his/her lifetime. There is the sense of being carried along on a river of sympathy in bereavement. There are the many practical touches of care and concern. People are tender and understanding. The funeral itself is an important step in the grieving process. The presence of the body and the last farewell before burial or cremation bring a certain sense of completion at that stage.

It is infinitely harder for those who have to do their grieving in the absence of an actual body, to come to terms with death. Those who cannot bid farewell to the physical remains of a loved person because the body has never been recovered after a drowning or mountaineering accident, an air crash, fire or, worse still, one of those unsolved disappearances where death has to be assumed but can never be established. Grieving is a very merciful thing, but if the process is interrupted, stopped or 'frozen', as it was for Mary when she discovered the absence of the body, it brings not only shock but shockingly intense pain.

Once a funeral is over, however, and the friends and relations have gone, there is a sudden cessation of urgent things to do. Then it is that the awareness of the empty place can hit hard. Often at the same time that the initial numbness begins to wear off, there comes a reduction in the flow of sympathy. It is a struggle to pick up the pieces of life and return to normality.

This must have been something of Mary's experience too. The hours of that Sabbath when Jewish law forbad them to return to the tomb to minister the last loving rites upon the body, must have been bleak. Perhaps the women shared together the rich memories they had of Jesus, wept together, consoled one another, comforted the disciples, and made their plans for their early morning visit to the tomb.

For Mary there was still the promise of that last look upon the face of the Lord, a last opportunity to minister to him in practical ways. Probably she had got no further than that in her thinking. She had not faced, at that stage, the loss she would feel once the stone was rolled in front of the tomb finally and permanently. She may not have thought what she would do after that, where she would go – whether or not she would stay on in Jerusalem or return to Magdala.

We can, therefore, enter into her sense of deep and terrible shock when she discovers that the body has gone. The relief that the stone had already been removed from the mouth of the tomb is not uppermost, the words of the young men who are sitting in the tomb don't seem to have penetrated. (Why are they there anyway? Were they the ones sent to move the body and now have returned to 'tidy up'? And why are the grave clothes lying there instead of being on the body of the Lord? Was it necessary to remove them in order to transfer the body to a different tomb? What right had they to interfere?) A confusion of questions may have filled her mind. One thing seems obvious; she has noted the absence of the body but not grasped the implications. Nor has she 'received' what the young men have said. Her pain acts as a block. All she can grasp are the words, 'He is not here'. Well then, where is he? Where can she start looking? She is fast running out of energy after the trauma of the past three days, and she weeps.

Liturgically, Mary Magdalen is often linked with the woman in the Song of Songs who sought her loved one but could not find him. She ran round the city asking people, 'Have you seen him whom my soul loves?' Every time the elusive lover appears to the distraught woman – knocking on the door, peering through the window – and she thinks she has got him in her grasp, he slips away like a will o'

the wisp, and she is desolate. The search begins all over
again. She vows that when she finds him she will hold him
and will not let him go.

In their experience of loss, the woman in the Song of
Songs and Mary Magdalen together provide a symbol of
a necessary stage in Christian growth.

Every Christian in the process of maturing at times
experiences the loss of Christ. There is no longer a sense
of his presence. He has 'disappeared'. They can identify
with Mary's pain for they too have known times when, 'He
is not here.' 'Where is the blessedness I knew when first I
saw the Lord?' wrote one hymnwriter, as though the test
of one's spiritual health lay in a sustained, warm glow of
the felt presence of Jesus from early days on. Doubtless we
can all look back to a period of marvellous, initial fervour
in our Christian walk, or in our vocation, when we were
'crazed with love' and the fire of ardour burned brightly.
We need to take heed, however. That fire can burn out
through inanition. If it has not been sufficiently fuelled, it
will die. That accounts for quite a number of 'drop outs'
amongst new converts. But for those who remain faithful
there also comes a time when they feel a devastating but
inescapable sense of loss. The fire *seems* to have gone out
in them. The worship, the books, the hymns, the fellowship
that once took them to the heights now leave them cold.
Sermons no longer seem to 'speak', prayer becomes a drag,
they are sustained solely by a curious pull – a desire for
God. And then, maybe, even that goes.

All too little teaching is given to encourage those who
have reached this stage, to assure them that it is actually
growth. After the starry-eyed idealism – which is the starting
place for most of us – comes the point at which the Spirit
of truth enters to dissolve it in the necessary and Christian
process of disillusionment; 'for illusions, whether about
God, other people or oneself must be smashed if a Christian
is to grow to full maturity'.[2]

Dependence upon feelings must go too; but all too often

the loss of feelings is equated with a loss of Christ himself.
Stripped of our illusions, stripped of feelings, stripped of
consolations, we may be plunged into mourning our loss.
Yet, it is then that we begin to learn the true meaning of
hope. Hope is certainty based on faith.

> Supernatural hope is the virtue that strips us of all things
> in order to give us possession of all things. We do not
> hope for what we have. Therefore to live in hope is to
> live in poverty having nothing . . . By faith we know God
> without seeing him. By hope we possess God without
> feeling his presence . . . The only thing faith and hope
> do not give us is the clear vision of him whom we possess.
> We are united to him in darkness, because we have to
> hope.[3]

The death and resurrection of Jesus were, for Mary
Magdalen, a doorway into a new dimension of relationship
with her beloved Lord. To walk through that door was to
discover the virtues of faith, hope and love, for, 'Faith is
the substance of things hoped for, the evidence of things
not *seen* . . .' (Heb 11:1).

'Hope that is seen is not hope. For who hopes for what
he sees? But if we hope for what we do not see, we wait
for it with patience' (Rom 8:24–5).

'Love bears all things, believes all things, endures all
things, love never ends . . . For now we see in a mirror
dimly, but then face to face. Now I know in part; then I
shall understand fully . . .' (1 Cor. 13:7–8, 12).

'Sin sets boundaries to our hope and locks our love in
prison,'[4] and it was to set Mary free that Jesus was 'not
here' – the elusive loved one who had 'gone before' into
resurrection, into a dimension of being where he would be
bound by nothing, other than man's utter refusal to love.

'Detachment' the Fathers called this experience of love.
It does not mean a total loss of feeling for ever. Nor should
we deny or despise feelings. Such saints as Ignatius of
Loyola and Theresa of Avila stressed the importance of

feelings and the need to be in touch with them. It does, however, imply a freedom from dependence on them.

> We live in a very existential age. The value of many courses of action is judged on whether or not it feels good. And that attitude has spilled over to Christians . . . If our Christian life depended on our feelings we should be in a real mess. Facts, faith, feelings should be kept strictly in that order . . . This cult of religious feelings is quite harmful to true Christian discipleship.[5]

Feelings have their place, they serve a purpose, they are a gift. But they must never be a crutch. Nor must we allow their subjectivity to overrule the objectivity of Christian truth.

The experience of loss does not, however, apply only or even chiefly to feelings. The loss which keeps us seeking 'him whom our soul loves' is the loss of knowing, the loss of certainty. We are plunged into darkness, into bewilderment, into a cloud of unknowing. Even the assurance that this is part of growth does not remove the pain of the loss. We stand weeping at the tomb, not only mourning lost religious feelings but at the seeming loss of Christ himself. At the centre of our being there is a great empty ache.

We are in the darkness of bewilderment. Like the woman in the Song of Songs, we cast around looking for him here and there in the familiar and known – the books we love, the favourite passages of Scripture, the music that once had power to stir us, in prayer groups and retreats. (Oh the desperate feeling of those retreats when, instead of gathering nourishing food for our journey as we had hoped, instead of a vital encounter with the Lord, we were confronted with an awful nothingness).

An essential aspect of our purification in prayer is the quiet acceptance of this enigmatic emptiness that foils all our plans and leaves us at a loss to know for certain

whether or not we have a spiritual life to worry about
. . .[6]

Why, we may wonder, should this kind of experience be
a necessary part of growth? Should not God do everything
in his power to encourage rather than discourage, clear the
path rather than put stumbling blocks in our way, water
our desire instead of seemingly quenching it?

The answer of course has to do with the need for the
purging of desire. If Mary had been able to analyse her
tears, how much would she have had to acknowledge that
they were due to a sense of very personal loss, a desire to
enjoy Jesus for herself, a desperate longing to cling to
what she had known of Jesus so far rather than waiting
expectantly to discover him in new ways?

So too, as we mature in prayer, we need the courage to
accept, when stuck at our particular point of growth, that
'He is not here'.

He is not going to 'mark time' in order to give us a false
sense of security. 'He goes before,' he is ahead preparing
the way, ever drawing us onward.

> With the drawing of this Love and the voice of this
> 　　Calling
> We will not cease from exploration[7]

either in prayer, or in our growth into God.

Only complete detachment from concerns about our
personal spiritual progress, only freedom from dependence
upon 'certain techniques that feed the birds of appetite'[8]
will enable us to continue seeking and finding God, and
finding him in all things, not just through my subjective
experience of him.

> It is a greater thing and a better prayer to live in Him
> who is Infinite and to rejoice that He is Infinite, than to
> strive always to press His infinity into the narrow space
> of our own hearts. As long as I am content to know that
> He is infinitely greater than I and that I cannot know

Him unless He shows Himself to me, I will have peace, and He will be near me and in me, and I will rest in Him. But as soon as I desire to know and enjoy Him for myself, I reach out to do violence to Him who evades me, and in so doing I do violence to myself and fall back upon myself in sorrow and anxiety, knowing that He has gone His way.[9]

He will not permit those experiences and those devotional aids, that initially led us into relationship with him, to trap him or us at a fixed point along the way. He will not be bound by the grave clothes with which we attempt to immobilise and control him, nor become encapsulated in the tomb by our fear.

Peter made the mistake that many of us make when we come into some new and overwhelming experience of the Lord. This is *IT*, we feel. This is great. Never have we known such joy, wonder, delight and desire. We have 'arrived' spiritually. Why should we move from this spot? We must hang on to this experience for dear life.

On the Mount of Transfiguration, Peter was overcome by this very fear of losing the experience. Wanting desperately to 'fix' the Lord (and Moses and Elijah) in that moment of wonder, enshrine the divine glory in a dwelling place 'made with hands', he offered to build three booths as a way of housing the wonder of it all in perpetuity. He, too, was striving to press Infinity into a narrow space. He wanted to encapsulate the revelation and use it as a museum piece to remind him of former and 'better' times, of the 'great' moment. 'Lord, it is good to be here. Let us build . . .'

But what is the point? The Lord is suddenly 'not here'. A cloud descends as it did upon Peter, James and John . . . and the moment has passed. The Lord has gone on before, beckoning us to follow and to encounter him in mystery. We are pilgrims on a journey, not permitted to settle into the security of the known. Always we have to turn away resolutely from the bondage of a neurotic clinging to past or present experiences, in order to follow the one who 'goes before'.

> He is such a fast God,
> always before us
> and leaving as we arrive.[10]

That is the essence of discipleship.

But the 'He is not here,' is accompanied by 'Do not be afraid'. We have not really lost him – only failed to capture him and pin him down. Just as the crowd, who came to seize Jesus, were left holding the cloth that had been wrapped around the 'young man who fled' from them (Mark 14:51), so we are left holding a grave cloth whilst the free and risen Christ dances on ahead calling us to stop forcing him to go at our pace, indulging in too lengthy a resting place along the way or mistakenly seeing the graces and consolations as the goal and journey's end. They are but the moments when the divine light becomes visible. For much of the time the light of God is a dazzling darkness that leads us into humility and dependence upon him. Stumbling and groping in the excessive light of his glory, we feel blind and reach out for his hand. In the moments that *feel* like light we become confident and, all too often, over-confident. 'Lord it is good to be here, at this particular point in my growth. Let us stop here for a while, raise an altar, build a shrine and hang on to the certainties of what I can see and feel.'

Our pleas are ignored as Peter's were, for our Courteous Lord (as Mother Julian loved to call him) neither makes an issue of our folly nor allows us to be imprisoned in it. He calls us on and out to expand the horizons that have become cramped by fear, to show us vistas of unimaginable beauty that spring out of the darkness.

Bewildering as it all seems at the time, it is actually in the darkness that most of our growing is done. The rule in the natural world – growth in the darkness of the soil, growth in the darkness of the womb – applies to the spiritual too. Thomas Merton was able to testify that 'remaining in His darkness has fed me and made me to grow'.[11]

It is painful, of course, as it was for Mary Magdalen. In facing the darkness, sometimes prolonged periods of it, we should acknowledge the pain, allow it to *be* pain and not seek to call it by other names. We need to admit that it is not easy.

> There is no consolation. There is no relief. There is no hope certain; the whole system is a mere illusion. I, who hope so much, and am so rapt up in the soul, know full well that there is no certainty. The tomb cries aloud to us – its dead silence presses on the drum of the ear like thunder, saying, 'Look at this, and erase your illusions.'[12]

We may well share this sense of hopelessness and illusion. To continue at all requires courage, big-heartedness and the generosity that Ignatius stressed so much upon those who set out on the road of his Spiritual Exercises. Of one thing we can be certain. God will not be outdone in generosity. He calls us to enter the darkness in order to discover him in new ways, in order to grow. We cannot see, we do not feel, we no longer know but, as St Bernard assures us, 'God can never be sought in vain, not even when he cannot be found.'[13]

The Christian spiritual tradition has been rich in its exponents of the way of divine dark. Gregory of Nyssa has been called 'the father of Christian mysticism'. His influence was immense upon the Apophatic tradition, and its subsequent followers. In this particular path of mysticism, his immediate discipline was Dionysius the Areopagite, and later St John of the Cross. Briefly the theology of negation, the doctrine of darkness, the Via Negativa, teaches that

God is so utterly different from anything or anyone we know, the love of God is so different from anything we have experienced, the glory of God is such a dazzling and blinding light, that as we approach God our dazed faculties, unable to endure the sight, are plunged into the most radical darkness. Just as the bat is blinded by the intense light of the sun, so we are blinded by the intense light of God. We do have a vision of God (as Moses had a vision of God) but we see him in the darkness. We see him through faith. In naked faith this dark vision of God is filled with mystical suffering,[14]

for we mainly experience it as an appalling aridity, anguish and deprivation. Faith becomes a dark, dark vision of God in which, like Moses too, we enter the cloud.

'The Cloud of Unknowing' aptly describes this way of prayer in which we may be tempted to think that prayer is futile and that we are unsupported by God. The advice given to climbers is to 'stay put' when a cloud descends. It is hazardous to continue climbing when it is impossible to see more than a footstep ahead. In the *Cloud of Unknowing* there is certainly a passivity, but it is active passivity. We are always moving, following in the footsteps of the Lord who has gone before. Prayer is not static. We are not 'blocks of wood to be carved on', as de Caussade reminds us. We are not marking time fruitlessly. We are forced to use such images as 'cloud' and 'darkness' as the only ones appropriate to describe our experience but we cannot press the analogies too far. They serve as handmaids of the Lord to the mystic to try and explain the inexplicable. Human language is incapable of describing fully the mystical experience of darkness in which there is 'a knowledge beyond discourse and vision beyond images'. Though such knowledge is frequently described as darkness, we are also assured, that at the 'heart of our abandonment in the spiritual night' there is a 'wholly other kind of apprehension, which so enables us *to find our way around in the dark* that the heart of darkness itself becomes bright'.[15] (Italics mine).

Hence there is a movement, progress, and a courageous 'going on' in the darkest night. We need not fear the dark even when it seems to be the loss of everything we ever gained in prayer. 'For his sake I have suffered the loss of all things, and count them as refuse, in order that I may gain Christ and be found in him . . . that I may know him and the power of his resurrection' (Phil. 3:8–10).

There are enough allusions in the Epistles to suggest that Paul himself was a mystic (or certainly knew mystical experiences in prayer). Maybe these well-known, much loved words in his letter to the Philippians refer to this aspect of loss, as well as to material and physical loss.

This was the loss Mary Magdalen was beginning to experience. This was the 'finding' that Jesus desired for her – a 'knowledge of him that was beyond discourse', an experience of the power of resurrection beyond senses and reason.

> Lord Jesus Christ, let me seek you by desiring you,
> and let me desire you by seeking you,
> let me find you by loving you,
> and love you in finding you . . .[16]

All such knowledge is gift. It is not acquired by techniques, skills, self-conscious forms of renunciation. We do not enter the darkness by willing it. It is not a matter of desire or planned enterprise.

We come to the tomb of our hopes drawn only by love; and the emptiness we find is a gift of pure love for our highest good. Jesus will come to us in our darkness, in the emptiness. Most assuredly he will. There *is* respite in the darkness as François Fénèlon said, 'This state of trouble and darkness, which is but for a while, hath ever its peaceful respites, flashes of grace illuminating the black night of the storm and leaving no trace behind them.'[17]

The Lord will come but it may be as the stranger – as

he came to his apostles. He is the stranger on the shore, the stranger on the road, the stranger at the tomb and 'eludes identification and control'.[18] He comes to us in sovereign freedom and he goes before with divine and glorious liberty, calling us out on to the frontiers of new experience and deeper relationship with him. We accept the darkness, we shed our tears at the seeming loss of all things, we cannot say that he is 'here' or 'there'.

We only know that in the darkness we *shall* hear his words, 'Fear not, for I have redeemed you; I have called you by name, you are mine' (Isa. 43:1).

'Mary!'

She turned and said to him, 'Rabboni!'

As he shatters our darkness and despair, calling us by name, we breathe out *our* one-word response in a moment of pure joy. At that moment we know that we have 'gained him' who is the ALL. His claim is total. Our finding is complete.

O Christ, my Lord, again and again
I have said with Mary Magdalene,
'They have taken away my Lord
and I know not where they have laid him.'
I have been desolate and alone.
And thou hast found me again, and I know
that what has died is not thou, my Lord,
but only my idea of thee,
the image which I have made to preserve
what I have found, and to be my security.
I shall make another image, O Lord, better than the
    last.
That too must go, and all successive images,
until I come to the blessed vision of thyself,
O Christ, my Lord.

(George Appleton)[19]

1. Charles Elliott, *Praying the Kingdom* (Darton, Longman and Todd 1985), p. 32.
2. From a review by Derek W. Allen of *The Choice* by Sister Kirsty (Hodder 1982), in *Fiat*, vol. 2, p. 72. *Fiat* is the now discontinued journal of the Community of St Mary the Virgin.
3. Thomas Merton, *No Man is an Island* (Hollis and Carter 1955), p. 11.
4. Ibid., p. 15.
5. Michael Green, *Baptism: Its Purpose, Practice and Power.* (Hodder 1987), p. 119.
6. James Finley, *Merton's Palace of Nowhere* (Ave Maria Press 1978), p. 100.
7. T. S. Eliot. 'Little Gidding' (Four Quartets), *Collected Poems 1909–1962* (Faber 1963), p. 222.
8. Finley, *Merton's Palace of Nowhere*, p. 91.
9. Ibid., p. 78.
10. R. S. Thomas, 'Pilgrimages', *Frequencies* (Macmillan 1978), p. 51.
11. Thomas Merton, *The Sign of Jonas* (Burns and Oates 1961), p. 184.
12. Richard Jefferies, *The Story of My Heart* (Longmans 1907), ch. XI.
13. St Bernard of Clairvaux, cited by E. Herman in *The Meaning and Value of Mysticism* (James Clarke 1915), p. 187.
14. William Johnston, *Christian Spirituality Today* (Collins 1984), p. 5.
15. Patrick Grant, *A Dazzling Darkness* (Collins 1985), p. 223 (italics mine).
16 St Anselm, cited in *An Oxford Book of Prayer*, ed. George Appleton (OUP 1985), p. 68.
17. François Fénèlon, *Maxims of the Mystics*, Article IX.
18. Rowan Williams, *Resurrection* (Darton Longman and Todd 1982), p. 43–4.
19. *The Oxford Book of Prayer*, no. 498.

5

Space to Dance

The power of freedom

I found him whom my soul loves. I held him, and would not let him go. . . .
                                                          (Song of Sol. 3:4)

Only when we are able to 'let go' of everything within us, all desire to see, to know, to taste and experience the presence of God, do we truly become able to experience that presence with the overwhelming conviction and reality that revolutionise our entire inner life.

(*Thomas Merton*)[1]

To the doubting Thomas Jesus said, 'Touch me,' and to the ecstatic Mary Magdalen, 'Touch me not.' To the one there was the invitation to cleave to him in faith rather than depend on visible and tangible evidence. To the other there was the invitation to create a space in order to grow in relationship, a call to greet the unexpected, to move on from a dependence on physical presence, from the desire to trap and be trapped in the known and familiar, to deepen in love, to find security in unknowing. Hence the apparent contradiction.

Let us try and reconstruct the scene. It is early in the morning. Maybe Mary hasn't slept much. Grief has kept her awake. She cannot begin to cope with the memory of that excruciating death she witnessed two days before. There has not been the necessary time or emotional space for the memories even to have begun to heal. Nor has she been able to deal with the confusion of feelings she has about the soldiers who carried out the execution. They were simply doing their normal work, of course. They were not personally involved. Jesus was just another prisoner condemned to die – there had been so many others. It was always such a long drawn out, boring affair. They grew sick of the screams of agony, the curses, the ever-weakening cries as the prisoners drew near to death. They had no option but just to sit it out. Dicing was one way of whiling away the hours. This time there had been the additional interest of a handsome robe at stake. Too good to divide up between them, they had gambled for it – right before the eyes of the one for whom it had been made by loving hands, the one who had worn it and hallowed it by his use.

Mary cannot get over their callousness, their indifference to suffering or to the feelings of the prisoner, their total lack of sensitivity, the coldness in their eyes, their uncouth speech and coarse laughter. Were these men who would go home and tenderly play with their children and love their wives? Would their families be proud of this day's work? When it came to the hour of their own death, could these men remember the way they had treated their victims? They could not escape performing their duty, but it could have been done with some respect, some milk of human kindness.

Weary, sick at heart, cold from lack of sleep and food, she rises early and joins the other women, to make the pilgrimage to the tomb in Joseph of Arimathea's garden. She knows there will be yet another set of guards. Word has got around that the religious authorities are in such a state of anxiety about this death, they have managed to put pressure on Pilate to set a watch over the tomb. Well, *she* must try and handle any arguments there are, and spare the others the pain of encountering their hostility and abusiveness. Maybe her thoughts were centred so much on how she was going to coax and persuade the soldiers to be lenient, she had scarcely given any thought to the major problem of how they were to get entrance to the tomb – how they were going to break the Governor's seal and roll away that massive stone. Getting to the garden, being close to all that was left of Jesus was what preoccupied her thoughts and drove her on through her weariness. She had already once before, on that previous memorable occasion, anointed him and he had seen it as a rehearsal for his burial. On that occasion she had performed the act in tears. Now, it is the real thing – a second anointing and, despite all her efforts to check them for the sake of others, especially his mother, there are more tears.

Only as they drew near did the women become really bothered about the obstacles that lay ahead. 'Who will roll away the stone for us?' they said. And then . . . suddenly, all is confusion. The guards are not there, the stone is already rolled away, the body has gone and there are strange men telling them that Jesus is 'not here. He is risen and goes before you to Galilee.'

In Matthew's Gospel an earthquake takes place *as* Mary Magdalen and the other Mary arrive at the sepulchre. It seems they were present as 'the angel of the Lord descended from heaven and rolled back the stone and sat on it . . .' It was then that 'for fear of him the guards trembled' and passed clean out with shock. The women are told not to be afraid. 'He is not here, he is risen as he said, but come and see the place where he lay' (Matt. 28:6).

In Mark, Luke and John, the earthquake has already taken place when the women arrive, the stone is already rolled away, there is no mention of the guards passing out – or, indeed, of them still being around – and men in dazzling garments appear, or are already seated in the tomb, telling them the same thing, 'He is not here – he is risen (as he told you he would be),' and, 'He goes before you into Galilee.' In other words, 'Hurry back to Galilee to rendezvous with the risen Christ.'

As in all genuine eye-witness accounts there are some discrepancies in the relating of the facts. Bearing in mind that the accounts were written at least thirty years after the events, and in two cases at second hand, it is not surprising that there are slight variations. All those involved that day were in a state of confusion, shock, fear, delight and joy, and would not have recounted their experience in a methodical way as though giving witness in a court of law. It would all have come tumbling out in their need to share the news.

On one thing however, all four gospel writers are agreed. Mary Magdalen was amongst those who went to the tomb. The Gospels differ over 'the others'. In Matthew it is Mary Magdalen and 'the other Mary'. In Mark, it is Mary Magdalen and Mary the mother of James, and Salome. In Luke it is 'the women who had come with him from Galilee' (Luke 23:55) and 'Mary Magdalen and Joanna and Mary, the mother of James and the other women with them . . .' 'Luke 24:10). John's Gospel depicts Mary Magdalen coming alone to the tomb. (Did she remain behind when the others had left? Did she come back a second time on her own?)

Now in addition to her numbness, grief, and exhaustion, Mary is faced with a terrible bewilderment. She has lost even the little she had. Somehow she had clung to those last rites that she was going to perform as something which would still enable her to have some contact with the physical body of Jesus. She desperately needed to be able to re-enact that loving gesture of anointing which she had previously performed for him with costly perfume and, in the repetition, to hear his voice saying again in those compassionate tones, 'Leave her alone. She has done a beautiful thing.' She is a very physical person. So she needs to express her love in physical, tangible services – even in this moment of extremity.

And now she is robbed even of that opportunity. 'They' have taken the body away.

Where? Where have they taken it? (If there had been an answer to that she would undoubtedly have dashed off to try and move it, even single-handed!)

Who has taken it? Would they have handled him reverently?

Perhaps we have known the disappointment of going to
the airport to say 'Goodbye' to someone leaving the country
for some years. We have comforted ourselves with the
thought of a last farewell and then have arrived to find
they have already gone through to the departure lounge
and our opportunity for a last glimpse, a few last words,
has gone. If we multiply that disappointment a hundred,
even a thousand-fold, we begin to get some insight into
Mary's anguish. After the bitter sorrow of the trial and
death of her beloved Lord, this is just the last straw.

No wonder she stood at the tomb weeping. Thank goodness she could! The flow of tears would have released a
healing to her. They would have relaxed the taut nerves
rapidly reaching breaking point, and eased the broken
heart. These tears were necessary. Until they were shed
she was not able to 'hear' what these strange young men
in their dazzling garments were saying. She could not grasp
and assimilate the good news they gave. Acute inner pain
can sometimes make the eyes and ears of the heart blind
and deaf.

So, she stands weeping outside the tomb – perhaps it is
the first time she has been alone and free really to give
way to her tears. Then, there is a movement behind her.
There seem to be quite a number of strangers around at
the moment, the two inside the tomb and now this one. It
is all so bewildering she isn't at all clear why they are here
and what their purpose is, but presumably they are all
employees of Joseph of Arimathea, men who work for him
on his estate.

'My dear, why are you weeping? Whom are you trying
to find?' says the voice – a very kind voice. He is obviously
not going to order her out of the garden and accuse her of
trespassing. If he *is* the gardener, he may recognise her as
being one of those who came on Friday evening to
accompany the body on its last journey; who sat opposite
the sepulchre watching as the necessary formalities were
observed; who noted the place where they had laid him.

If anyone knows where the body has been taken this man will. He must be one of the more senior members of Joseph's household – perhaps the head gardener?

'Sir,' she says, 'if you have taken him to some other place, please tell me so that I can go and take him away.'

That's all that matters. I must get him. As long as I can find him . . . I'll sort out later how we are going to move these heavy jars with their ointment, oils and aromatic spices to the new tomb. They are too heavy for me to carry alone – besides which, it would slow me down and the only really important thing at the moment is to FIND HIM.

And then the voice – this time a rich, familiar, dearly loved voice – speaks again, simply saying, 'Mary'.

Her name! Her own name! And spoken in a way that was unique. Only ONE PERSON ever speaks her name just like that . . . 'RABBONI!' (Was it a shriek, a stifled sob, a whisper of unbelief, a cry of joy? Haven't we all tried to imagine it? Isn't it difficult trying to decide how to say it when asked to read this passage in public. A flat, unemotional voice is clearly inappropriate. But *how* – how did she respond? It is good that we don't know; good that Mary had this most special of all moments entirely to herself; right that there were no witnesses or eaves droppers – probably even the two young men inside the tomb would have left once Jesus appeared, since their purpose would have been served, their mission accomplished.)

'Rabboni!' and a leap forward. Here he is – in very flesh and blood standing beside me. Surely I can't be dreaming?

And then the grab, the flinging of the arms around him, the holding on, the joyful clutching by one who is terrified of losing the loved one again.

'Touch me not. Don't hold on to me,' he says – not because he is a ghost with an insubstantial body which cannot be held. Not because of any possible impropriety at a woman flinging her arms around a man. No. The meaning comes out quite clearly.

'Don't cling to me, Mary.'

'But, Lord,' she might well have thought, 'I was about to go searching for this very body of yours, to anoint it and prepare it for burial, and here you are in it, walking around ALIVE. I am so afraid you will disappear again. And *then* where do I start looking? I want you to stay. I want to hang on to this moment . . .'

There it is again – the same desire to enshrine a particular and special experience as, we have already noted, Peter had on the Mount of Transfiguration. Mary needed to learn, as Peter did, that vision is meant to be the quick matter of a dynamic relationship – not an heirloom.

How many of *us* have dealt a death blow to maturity and freedom in a relationship by desperately trying to encapsulate it in past patterns or the present state of affairs? How many mothers have clung to the childhood past of their adolescent (or even older) offspring, demanding a childish dependence which the sons or daughters struggle to outgrow and from which they *should* be freed. Hard as it may be for parents to live through that period of ambivalence in their children's lives, when they come running to mother one minute and seem to reject her the next, when they resent any seeming lack of interest or concern in their affairs, but equally can't tolerate parental interference, the letting go is essential.

Selfhood begins in the walking away
And love is proved in the letting go,

were words which came to C. Day Lewis as he walked back along the platform at the railway station where he had just seen his small son off to his prep. school. 'Walking away' and 'letting go' are essential to a mature relationship, but too often we fear them because initially they are experienced as loss. We are frightened of letting go our securities as we have known them. We want only the tried paths and cannot bring ourselves to explore uncharted areas of life. Clinging becomes a sin when we refuse to let go of our sacred images for deeper and more transcendent experiences. Our self-limitation becomes crippling. 'Sin,' said Gregory of Nyssa, 'is ultimately a refusal to grow.'[2]

Jesus certainly wanted to lead Mary into the freedom of a relationship that did not depend upon outward contact, but rather relied upon the kinship of spirits and the communication of the heart. He wanted her to transcend the old relationship with its limitations and discover him anew as the rise, free Christ. He had just broken out of the tomb. He did not want to walk straight into another form of burial, to be entombed in a hysteric's need to cling, which would never leave emotional space in the friendship. Possessiveness imposes restraints on loving. He wanted her to know the perfect love that casts out fear – especially the fear born of a wrong dependence.

Have you ever found yourself wondering why Jesus appeared first to Mary Magdalen rather than to his mother? Would it not have seemed appropriate to seek to comfort the one who, in his death, had suffered more than any other human being?

We cannot, of course, plumb that divine secret fully. It is obviously very significant that the disciples first heard of the resurrection through a woman (in view of contemporary attitudes to women at that time). 'Go quickly and tell his disciples and Peter that he is risen from the dead and behold, he is going before you to Galilee . . .' (Matt 28:7, Mark 16:7 amalgamated), the women are instructed by the angels of the tomb. After her encounter Mary did as she was bidden and promptly ran to the disciples. Can't we just picture it . . . the excitement, the laughing and crying together, the joy at bearing a message she believes will dispel their grief and pain. Her face afire, eyes sparkling, voice ringing she bursts in on them with, 'I have seen the Lord!'

I picture Mary as an energetic, vivacious, outgoing extrovert, but also someone who could be easily wounded, quickly dashed or flattened. The unbelief of the disciples is to her incredible. 'I suppose they think it has all been too much for me, my balance of mind has been disturbed, my reason impaired,' she must have wondered. Zefferelli showed great insight when, in his film *Jesus of Nazareth*, he portrayed Mary rounding on the disciples in a fury born of desperation, wiping the floor with them for being so sceptical and slow of heart. Her pain at not being believed or understood came across so vividly on the screen when, in the upper room, she broke the news to them and they treated it as an 'idle tale' (Luke 24:11).

Was it because Jesus recognised that *initially* women would be more receptive to the truth than men that he allowed Mary to be the first to bear the news of his resurrection? – to become the 'Apostle to the Apostles'.

Was it because of her immense generosity of heart that he appeared to her first? In the trial scene, Zefferelli showed her shouting for Jesus at the top of her voice against the crowd's deafening cry for Barabbas. Even when struck in the face by one of the political agitators, she never took her eyes off Jesus nor ceased to shout his name. And in the film, *his* eyes in turn missed nothing. He saw and heard her efforts to support him, even save him. The pain, gratitude and love all shone from his eyes as he watched her take the blows. It would have been so natural to want to 'reward' that kind of loyalty, a particularly poignant loyalty in the face of the desertion by his disciples.

Maybe, however, there is another reason why Mary Magdalen, and not his mother, was given priority in the resurrection appearances. His mother had already learned the depth of relationship possible in 'letting go'. She had already let her son go when he left home and his trade as a carpenter in order to be a peripatetic rabbi with a group of disciples. She knew that it was the end of his life as village carpenter, that his hour had come, that he had judged God's timing in this. His public ministry had begun and he would not be returning – not to his home and his old and settled life at Nazareth.

She had already 'let go' when 'they' came to Jesus and

said, 'Your mother and your brothers and sisters are
outside,' and he asked, 'Who is my mother? Who are my
brothers and sisters?' She knew, and we know, that this
puzzling response was in no way a slight upon his family.
It was certainly not an indication that he was ashamed of
them, or refused to acknowledge them. It was not irritation
that they seemed to be shadowing him, checking on his
movements and keeping him within their sights. He simply
took this occasion as a teaching opportunity to show that
the claims of the Kingdom took precedence over even
family loyalties, that in the Kingdom, love is an inclusive
matter. All who 'hear me' and 'do my word are my brothers
and sisters and mother' (cf. Matt. 12:46–50). Even so –
even though she understood – there must still have been a
slight pang for Mary, as she realised more clearly than
ever that she must set him free, that she must not make
inappropriate demands upon him which might conflict
with the coming of the Kingdom, that there must not be
even the subtlest attempt to dominate or manipulate and
tie him to apron strings. Nothing must hinder him going
about his Father's business.

Being such a whole person herself, and therefore such a
free person, she could face it. She had been preparing him
since babyhood for the moment of separation. She had
been inwardly 'letting go' all along, perhaps especially
since that visit to Jerusalem and the Temple when Jesus
was twelve. 'Did you not know that I must be about my
Father's business?' he had asked. And she recognised that
his selfhood, dimly apprehending its divine mission, had
begun to 'walk away', and *her* love would be proved in the
letting go'. She accepted his growing maturity.

Finally, she had 'let go' when he had set his face to go
to Jerusalem. Both he and she knew the likely consequences. She did not clutch and cling to him, she did not
apply emotional pressure through her tears, she did not
stand in his way or implore him to consider *her* feelings.
No hint, of 'How could you do this to your mother?' She

didn't stop him; she followed him. She didn't oppose him; she supported him. She did not wallow in self-pity; she flowed out to him in empathy. Her love deepened with every passing day as she entered more fully into an understanding of the cost of his mission – but it did so in the face of physical absence and with due respect for the 'space' she must give him in her loving.

The Cross was the ultimate 'letting go'. For here was not only the 'letting go' of her own flesh and blood, her *son*, but of all her hopes for him. Did she look back to the day when Magi had visited him as a baby and seemed to have precognition of his Kingship, to the time when Simeon said, 'This child is set for the rise and fall of the nation'? Far from having such significance in their national history, he was dying in ignominy and failure. Her hopes that the religious leaders would have the scales taken from their eyes and perceive the truth, were crushed. Her hopes that the people who had 'heard him gladly' would support him were dashed. Her hope, that she would see the Kingdom not only inaugurated but realised, was not to be fulfilled. But she still 'let go'. And now, in his resurrection, the depth of their love, which had already weathered physical separation, would know no bounds in the bonds of the spirit. In this, she was without sin, for 'sin sets boundaries to our hope and locks our love in prison'.[3]

Mary Magdalen, however, was not nearly so secure in her relationship. And, as with all of us, he met her where she was in her particular stage of growth. He understood, he sympathised, he loved her for her ardour and all-outness. But he longed that she might know greater freedom in her loving. He desired for her a loving that was free from the constant fear of losing him. He wanted her to enter into an ever-deepening intimacy with him, but 'fear does not create the space where true intimacy can exist',[4] the space where growth can take place.

'Don't cling! I am not yet ascended to my Father.' It is almost as though he is persuading her to use this short period when, from time to time, he will still be visibly present, as a transition period of learning to 'let go' before his bodily form is removed altogether. He wanted her to be able to return from the inescapable 'letting go' that his Ascension would involve with the joy of knowing that nothing can separate us from the love of Christ ' . . . neither death, nor life, nor angels, nor principalities, nor things present, nor things to come, nor powers, nor height nor depth, nor anything else in creation . . .' (Romans 8:38–9).

'Don't cling to me, Mary', was an invitation to discover that their relationship had no need to be a *fearful* clinging to him on her part. Rather, it could be 'a free dance, allowing space' in which they could 'move forward and backward, form constantly new patterns, and see each other as always new'.[5]

What Jesus sought to teach Mary as he gently led her into new depths of relationship, we all need to learn. In any relationship if it is to be truly enriching, there must be 'space to dance'. All too often we fail to allow each other enough solitude – solitude of heart as well as physical solitude. Our fear tells us that togetherness is based on physical presence to each other, and complete openness. Whereas it is the safeguarding of physical and emotional space that will lead to genuine closeness. Moreover, everyone, within marriage or friendship, needs an inner enclosure, the door of which is open only to God. For deep intimacy in relationship requires an area of inviolable privacy.

Without the solitude of heart, the intimacy of friendship, marriage and community life cannot be creative. Without the solitude of heart our relationships with others easily become needy and greedy, sticky and clinging, dependent and sentimental, exploitative and parasitic . . .

The mystery of love is that it protects and respects the aloneness of the other and creates the free space where we can convert this loneliness into a solitude that can be shared. In this solitude we can strengthen each other by mutual respect, by careful consideration of each other's individuality, by our obedient distance from each other's privacy and by a reverent understanding of the sacredness of the human heart.[6]

When we learn with Mary not to cling in relationship, when we are free of the fear of losing one another, then we begin to learn the true meaning of intimacy which respects the space around another. The perimeter of this space is not 'a fine line between distance and closeness, but a field of movement in which the question of whether we are close or distant is no longer the guiding question.'[7]

Sing and dance together and be joyous,
but let each one of you be alone.
Even as the strings of the lute are alone
though they quiver with the same music.

Stand together yet not too near together
For the pillars of the temple stand apart,
and the oak and the cypress
grow not in each other's shade.[8]

The sticking point for most of us is that this fear stems from our wounds – for wounded and damaged we all are, whether it be from early childhood trauma, unsatisfactory relationships with parents, or later wounds in friendship or marriage. Whether or not they are wounds we recognise and own, or deeply buried, hidden wounds in the recesses of our subconscious, they all blight our freedom in relationship. These wounds often cause us to make impossible demands on others, demands which trap them in our preconceived expectations of them and make them feel a failure when they cannot fulfil our demands. *Their* personal space becomes eroded, and *we* feel let down, hurt and rejected. Obviously, the more whole we are in ourselves, the more space we can afford to give others but, ultimately,

'God alone is free enough from wounds to offer us a fearless space.'[9]

'Don't cling to me, Mary,' is the Lord's call to explore the possibility and the challenge of relationship based not on human togetherness but on a covenant in which he dances with us; and dancing requires space.

Newly burst from the tomb in an explosion of resurrection joy, the Lord calls us to share his resurrection freedom. 'Don't cling! Dance!' he calls to us, 'for I am Lord of the Dance – the Dancing God. Throw off your grave clothes of fear and come forth from your particular tomb. Don't lay hold of me as a possession to be grasped.'

Yet, 'that is the tragic paradox. Love that is offered to make people free is so overpowering that it is quickly encased, and thereby robs people of the very freedom it was destined to secure. . .'[10]

Even though we may be deeply aware of our need for a transformation of attitudes, 'we neuter the one source of power that would make that transformation possible,'[11] if we grasp and cling.

'Step out into space,' he calls, 'and dance the dance of true intimacy.'

Dance then wherever you may be
I am the Lord of the Dance, said he
and I'll lead you all wherever you may be
And I'll lead you all in the dance, said he.[12]

1. Thomas Merton, *No Man is an Island* (Hollis and Carter 1955), p. 15.
2. Gregory of Nyssa, *From Glory to Glory*.
3. Thomas Merton, *No Man is an Island* (Hollis & Carter 1955), p. 15.
4. Henri Nouwen, *The House of the Lord* (Darton Longman and Todd 1986), p. 15.
5. Henry Nouwen, *Clowning in Rome* (Image Books 1979), p. 43.

6. Henri Nouwen, *Reaching Out* (Fount 1980), p. 44.
7. Nouwen, *The House of the Lord*, p. 20.
8. Kahlil Gibran, *The Prophet* (Heinemann 1926).
9. Nouwen, *The House of the Lord*, p. 23.
10. Charles Elliot, *Praying the Kingdom* (Darton Longman and Todd 1985), p. 64.
11. Ibid, p. 64.
12. Sydney Carter, 'Lord of the Dance' (Stainer & Bell 1963).

Epilogue

We have been following the spiritual pilgrimage of one person and have been indeed on holy ground. For we have been allowed to enter, perhaps more deeply than ever before, into Mary Magdalen's life-changing encounter with Jesus. It is tantalising not to know more of her personal history – her family background and childhood, and the subsequent ministry of this Apostle to the Apostles following the Ascension (tradition speaks of her missionary work as far afield as the south of France). But such information, though it would be interesting, is extraneous to the essential gift in the life story of Mary Magdalen. All that is recounted is richly nourishing in our own journey to God.

Mary Magdalen comes alive as a very real and warm person, sensitive, aware and capable of great compassion. She is no plaster saint on a pedestal, and we are therefore able to identify with her in her humanness and even perhaps in her earthiness. She provides for us something of a blueprint as we see the path to holiness through converted passion, wrought out of profound penitence. How can we remain unmoved by the reckless devotion and generosity of this woman? There is something so refreshingly robust about her faith. Captivated by this man, Jesus, who meets her where she is, loves her for who she is, accepts her as she is, and yet whose love and total forgiveness revolutionises her life, she goes flat out after him with only one desire – to give herself utterly to him in reciprocated love and devotion. Richard Rolle's words could equally be Magdalen's:

Jesus receive my heart and bring me to Thy love,
All my desire Thou art and Thy coming I covet.

Her desire, her love, her devotion were all harnessed as
one energy directed to Jesus.

Maybe through Mary Magdalen we are taken back to
early moments in our own faith-history – to poignant
memories of our 'first-love' when our ardour and zeal were
potent, our joy in forgiveness radiated from us and our
whole life took its meaning and direction from our relationship with Jesus. We wanted to 'lay our lives before him'.
With Mary Magdalen's ardent love before us, we may
reflect ruefully that subsequently we have grown weary,
the light in us burns a little more dimly and we have settled
for that dangerous state called 'spiritual plateau-ing'.
Reflecting on Mary Magdalen's all-or-nothingness may
have challenged our mediocrity, shattered our complacency
and rekindled the 'flame of sacred love on the mean altar
of our hearts'.

But, as we have seen, her story is not discouragingly
triumphalistic. We can identify with her fragility, her
devastation in the face of disappointment. Hopefully, if we
too have stood in a place of tears, weeping over a loss
which seems tragic and final, we can, through reflecting
on her journey to the empty tomb, enter into a more vital
experience of the Risen Lord and hear him say again to us
(almost as though he were just at our elbow): 'Fear not! I
have called you by name. You are mine.' And we spring
up from the depths with our own 'Rabboni'. We, too, feel
the need to cling to him – not in a neurotic paralysis of
fear, but because hand-in-hand with him we shall grow in
that perfect love which casts out fear, that love which both
transfigures us and frees us to find our true selves.

When the grey days come and the 'dark nights' of the
soul, when our spirits flag and we mourn the loss of former
spiritual consolations, this woman with her impetuosity
and vigour encourages us to search, to look into the empti-

ness, to face it squarely, to recognise that once more the Lord has eluded us as we looked for him in the expected place or way. But she points us to a radically new experience of resurrection where the grave of our hopes becomes the gateway to a new dimension of relationship with the Risen Jesus. We dry our tears, turn from our tombs and discover for ourselves the everlasting Easter of the Heart. It is the way of Mary Magdalen – the joyful journey she made from pain to passion, lust to love, fear to faith, doubt to dancing.